MICHAEL KEARNEY

WWJD?

Unlocking a Life Worth Living

LUCIDBOOKS

WWJD? Unlocking a Life Worth Living

Published by Lucid Books in Houston, TX
www.LucidBooks.com

ISBN: 978-1-63296-696-4
eISBN: 978-1-63296-697-1

Special Sales: Most Lucid Books titles are available in special quantity discounts. Custom imprinting or excerpting can also be done to fit special needs. Contact Lucid Books at Info@LucidBooks.com

TABLE OF CONTENTS

To my village: Dad, Mom, Nia, Trenton, and Zahrya, with a special thanks to my grandfather, William T. Caudle, who through death gave me life.

INTRODUCTION

What's up y'all!! Thank you for taking the time to read this book. I hope you enjoy reading it as much as I did writing it.

Cutting to the chase, I am going to start this off by giving you an overview of myself followed by the overall vision and structure for this book, some disclaimers, and a few closing comments.

About me: I am an Air Force veteran who loves sports and entertainment. When applicable, I incorporate this background to provide a modern context for the biblical principles discussed. As for my spiritual life, I was born and raised a non-denominational Christian. Though I was brought up in the church, I didn't develop my own personal relationship with God until 2018 when I was 22 years old. I believe it is important for all believers to discover God on their own because your faith and walk with God is a personal journey.

When you are brought up in the church like I was, it's like an arranged marriage. Your relationship with God is forced upon you. The way you interpret the teachings and guidelines of the Bible are dictated to you. There isn't much room for free thought or choice. I'm sure we've all had the experience of being dragged out of bed on Sunday and putting on that itchy suit or dress from the thrift store.

Going to church wasn't necessarily a fun thing we wanted to do. It felt like a chore, and I would be lying if I said there weren't *multiple* instances when I would have rather stayed home and watched cartoons while eating a bowl of cereal.

That is why finding God for yourself is so vital. We aren't kids being forced to wake up at 6:00 a.m. anymore. We have the choice between going to church and spending the day watching football. When you aren't told or encouraged to find God for yourself, it is easy to choose a day watching football because you have no intrinsic motivation to continue your walk with God. My hope is that those reading this will be encouraged to develop their own personal relationship with God or strengthen the one they already have.

Vision: My overall vision for this book is to create spiritual warriors who think critically about their faith and how their choices impact and touch the world around them.

Structure:

1. This book chronicles the events of Jesus's life as told in the Gospel of Matthew, with an emphasis on *events*. In church, we tend to focus on the *teachings* of Jesus. This book focuses on the things Jesus endured as a *man*. We will be diving into how Jesus lived His life and pulling lessons from the example He set so we can apply them to our own lives.
2. Each chapter is broken into four sections: Overview, Analysis, Conclusion, and Reflection Questions. The Overview gives a quick summary of the biblical text being covered. The Analysis dives into the lessons learned from the text. The Conclusion is the author's parting thoughts and key takeaways. The Reflection Questions are based on the content of the chapter and are used to provoke thought and facilitate discussion. There is space provided at the end of each

chapter of the hard-copy version for you to journal your responses.

3. Knowing you all are busy people, I've deliberately made each chapter "bite-sized," meaning there aren't any super text-heavy chapters. They should all be quick five-to-ten-minute reads.
4. As for the style, I wrote this book to read like a conversation. It reads how I talk. My goal is to talk *to* you and not *at* you.

Disclaimers:

1. Throughout the book I present several lessons. These lessons are what God has revealed to *me* during my walk with Him. That being said, I am in no way saying that what I believe is 100 percent right. In fact, I want to be challenged. I want you to disagree with me because disagreement means you have an opinion, and having an opinion means you are thinking critically about the text, which is the ultimate vision of this book.
2. Akin to point one, I don't intend for this to be a do-as-I-say book. I believe God speaks to each of us differently and that there are multiple ways to slice this cake called life. I bring this up because there are several chapters where I say, "Don't . . . blah blah blah." I phrase things this way because saying "don't" is much quicker than saying "I believe it would behoove you to refrain from _____" in every other sentence. It's not written to literally tell you what you should and shouldn't do. God gave us free will for a reason. Ultimately, it's not my job to tell you how to live your life. My job is to provide a perspective that sparks deeper introspection and conversation.
3. One of my personal goals when writing this was to be raw and authentic. How you read the text is how I interpreted the text organically. The examples and comparisons that are made are things I thought of as I was writing. It is not meant to say

"this person is on the same level as Jesus." It is only utilized to point out similarities between situations. It is not a one-to-one comparison.

4. As stated previously, this book reads how I talk. Therefore, it is not going to sound like the Christian literature you are accustomed to. I'm from the South, so there will be "y'alls," "ain'ts," and other slang sprinkled in. I ask that you focus on the *content* of the message and not how the message is presented. If you've ever done an elephant gift exchange, you know that some of the best gifts come from the most unsuspecting packages.
5. I understand that people will take issue with me making secular comparisons in a Christian book. My justification is this: Let's say the average Christian goes to church every Sunday. That's 52 out of 365 days in a year, which is 14.2 percent. That means in a calendar year, they spend 85.8 percent of their days in the secular world—99.4 percent if you break it down hourly (assuming church is one hour). From a logical perspective, how can we *not* talk about the real world when discussing faith when that is where we spend 99.4 percent of our time? My desire is to teach people how to operate as a Christian *within* the secular world.

Closing Comments: I'm not going to sit here and flex my PhD in Biblical Doctrine or talk about how I've been a pastor for 10 years because none of that is true. I'm just a regular guy with a passion for Christ—a sinner trying to be a saint. My only credentials are that I've read the whole Bible and spent some time ministering to recovering drug addicts in an unofficial capacity.

The reason I am telling you this is to illustrate the point that you don't need to be "certified" to make a difference. You don't have to wait until someone gives you a piece of paper stating you're qualified to do x, y, and z to change lives. As you will soon read, Jesus didn't recruit the most qualified individuals to be His disciples. He selected regular, everyday, and sometimes morally questionable dudes who were willing to give up everything to follow Him.

This tells me that we all possess the capability to be advocates and warriors for Christ if we choose to submit ourselves to Him.

That's all I've got for you. Have a blessed journey.

CHAPTER 1

FIND YOUR PURPOSE

Matthew 1:1–17

Overview:

I considered skipping this section due to the fact that it's one of those "this person begot that person, this person begettin' these people" genealogy-based chapters that doesn't have anything to do with the actions of Jesus Himself. However, after giving it deeper thought, I realized that analyzing the genealogy of Jesus from a macro scale provides a grander perspective on the age-old question: What is my purpose in life?

Analysis:

This will be broken into two parts. Part 1 is my outlook on purpose. Part 2 is a methodology for finding your purpose.

Part 1

When reading through the lineage of Christ, a lot of prominent biblical figures stick out—Abraham, Isaac, King David, Amon, Eliakim, and of course, Jeconiah. What? You aren't familiar with the last three names I mentioned? Oh. Yeah. That was by design and is used to illustrate the point that even though you the reader may not know the background of every individual in the 42 generations preceding Christ, their sheer existence was pivotal in the facilitation of His coming.

Allow that to sink in for a moment. *Forty-two* generations spanning *thousands* of years occurred prior to Jesus's birth. These people endured wars, famine, slavery, and all types of diseases in order to continue their bloodline, and one singular break in the chain would eradicate each generation thereafter.

Think about it like this: if the slave owners in the genealogy-based book *Roots* decided to kill Kunta Kinte for refusing to go by Toby, that would have been the end of *Roots*. There would be no story after that. I say all that to say… you matter. *You matter!* Your existence on this earth serves a greater purpose, and don't let anyone make you feel differently.

The world will try to sell you the idea that your purpose is tied to your social status and ability to elevate into a different tax bracket. It's not. In fact, Jesus teaches us not to store up our treasures on earth but in heaven with Him (Matt. 6:19–21). In other words, having 100,000 followers on Instagram isn't gonna punch your ticket into the pearly gates. Those $500 shoes aren't gonna buy your salvation.

Not everyone is meant to be a Barack Obama, Oprah Winfrey, Beyoncé, or LeBron James. Not everyone is meant to be multi-millionaires, own yachts, or be able to afford courtside seats to the Lakers game. Those are just facts. It's okay to desire those things, but don't think you failed in life just because you've never been behind the wheel of a Porsche. Don't get caught up in trying to achieve the world's standards of greatness—be great in your faith. Be great in your walk with God and ability to walk in the purpose He has laid out for you.

Conclusion:

Grow where you're planted. Be the best you can be where God has put you. Some of us are meant to be construction workers making an honest living for our families. Others are meant to be first-generation college graduates, showing the people coming after them what is possible to achieve. Maybe your purpose is to simply be a great parent to the kid who grows up to become President of the United States one day. You never know, but whatever your purpose is on this earth, it matters and influences all generations to come.

Part 2

How does one find their purpose? I've boiled it down to two key ingredients that work hand-in-hand—discernment and acceptance. You have to discern what may or may not be in God's plan for you and accept when He tells you what is.

Discernment is probably the most difficult because each of us has dreams, aspirations, and goals for our lives. However, as we all know, if you wanna make God laugh, tell Him about your "plans."

The fact that this is a well-known saying is proof enough that our purpose in life often falls outside of our personal desires, and in my experience, we tend to put on blinders and fixate on the things we want to do. That prevents us from seeing the bigger picture and prolongs the journey. Get out of your own way.

In the Air Force, we say flexibility is the key to airpower. We must be flexible with our ambitions. We must be willing and able to pivot our trajectory at the drop of a hat. God can hit us with our purpose at any moment, and we have to be ready to answer the call.

Acceptance seems like a no-brainer, but it can be extremely difficult if it's something you don't want to do. Cue my man Jonah (Jon. 1–4). That brotha is the *king* of dodging God's calling. God gave him *explicit* instructions to preach to the people of Nineveh. My man said "nah" and then literally got on a boat and set sail to a completely different city. In response, God had Jonah eaten by a whale where he essentially sat in timeout for three days until he learned his lesson.

As you would expect of someone who had just been eaten alive, Jonah ended up doing what God asked. He didn't like it though. In fact, he threw a whole tantrum when he found out God spared the people of Nineveh. He said, and I *directly* quote, "O Lord, please take my life from me, for it is better for me to die than to live!" (Jon. 4:3). Talk about melodramatic!

Moral of the story: don't be a Jonah. Accept God's calling willingly because whether you like it or not, it's gonna happen.

Now that I've told you the secret ingredients, I want to share how you can go about uncovering what God has for your life.

Before I dive in, allow me to reemphasize for those who didn't read the Introduction that anything I say is what God has communicated and revealed to *me*. That doesn't mean it will work for you or resonate with you. We are all different people, and I believe God communicates to each of us in individualized ways that resonate the best with our personalities. That said, it is important to pray, meditate, and ask God to guide you where He needs you to go. The below list includes actions and indicators you can utilize *in conjunction with* your prayer life.

Anyways, here's my list:

1. *Stop comparing*! If you noticed in the previous paragraphs, I never suggested that you should listen to Oprah or Steve Harvey to figure out what you need to be doing with your life. I said to listen to God—the big G-O-D.

We live in an era where we, more than ever, evaluate what we should be doing based on what we see others doing or saying on social media. We see all our friends from high school getting married or buying a house, and we think that's what we should be doing.

We see an influencer making millions of dollars doing a 15-second dance, and we consider giving up our $40,000-a-year emergency room technician job because it doesn't pay enough money.

Everywhere we turn we see the things we are *not* doing—ways we are *not* good enough, *not* fit enough, *not* attractive enough, *not* rich enough. *Turn that noise off!* It is directly impeding your ability to find God's purpose for you because you are inherently judging yourself by man's standards, and the desires and values of man rarely align with the will of God.

2. *Look for signs.* God will direct you where He needs you to go if you ask and allow Him to show you the way.

I once read a book called *Whisper: How to Hear the Voice of God.* In it, the author insinuates that God gives us "winks" to communicate messages. An example of this occurred the day after I began writing this chapter. God gave me the vision for this book, but I had a lot of doubt about whether or not what I had to say had value. In a very God-like fashion, the next day I had a casual conversation with a friend who, of his own volition, brought up Matthew Chapter 1 and the genealogy of Jesus—the very subject of this chapter.

Insane, right? The craziest part is that the conversation had nothing to do with my book or even religion! We were talking about cancel culture. If that isn't a sign, I don't know what is.

I firmly believe God gives us small whispers because that was the way He presented His Son to the world. Jesus wasn't born in the Ritz-Carlton. He didn't play trumpets and have dancers flanked around Him when He went into the city like Aladdin.

He was born in a manger and arrived into town on a donkey. He moved in subtle ways, so why wouldn't God communicate with us similarly? There will be instances where He sends you a whale like Jonah, but more often than not, you are going to have to open your third eye and decipher when God is communicating with you through other means.

3. *What lights your fire?* The ingredients I mentioned are geared towards when our desires *don't* align with God's plans, but there are times God blesses us with a passion that *does* align with His will. So if there is something you are deeply passionate about, chase after it—like the late and great Kobe Bryant.

From his youth, Kobe was all about basketball. This passion and drive led him to become one of the greatest players to ever play the sport. However, his purpose in life wasn't to become a basketball player. His purpose was to leave a legacy and a "Mamba Mentality" that inspires people to work obsessively hard at their goals and not allow fear to deter them from seizing their destiny. He did that *through* basketball. Unfortunately, he did not live to see the fruits of his labor, but I've come across many interviews of people who attribute their success to the legacy he left behind.

Sometimes you get to do the things you love, and God utilizes it as a vehicle to facilitate His will, so if you are one of the fortunate few who gets to live your dream, what are you doing with the blessing? How are you uplifting God's kingdom? Who are you impacting? Who are you inspiring or mentoring? Bringing all of this back to the theme of this book, Jesus didn't do things for the benefit of Himself. He did things to benefit the lives of others. He lived a life of service, and ultimately, that is what determines whether or not you are truly living your purpose—your ability to utilize your blessings in service to others.

Conclusion:

All in all, when I think of *purpose*, I think of life. People say that all life is precious, from the smallest amoeba to a blue whale. I believe everyone's purpose has value. You can impact millions, or you can impact a few. It all matters. You never know when a warm smile and a two-minute conversation will pull someone out of a dark place. You never know when your mere presence will make someone feel loved and supported. Be kind. Care. Do your best to live a life worth living. Finding your purpose can be a lifelong journey, but I want you to know before closing this chapter that you don't need to know your purpose to live your life purposefully. That, my friend, is completely up to you.

Reflection Questions:

After each chapter, there will be space for you to journal your thoughts and reflect on the discussion topic. You can write about anything you want, but I will provide reflection questions for those utilizing this book as a devotional or a Bible study, or if you just need a kick-start on what to write about.

1. What do you think your purpose is? Are you living it to the fullest?

____

____

____

____

2. If you don't know your purpose, what steps are you taking, and what steps will you take to find it?

3. What are the ways God has communicated His desires to you?

4. What prevents you from seeing yourself the way God sees you (social media, friends, family, etc.)? How are you going to improve on your self-perception?

5. When was the last time you had a positive impact on someone's life? How did you help them?

NOTES

CHAPTER 2

Be HUMBLE.

Matthew 3:13–16

Overview:

No, you are not at a Kendrick Lamar concert, but I do want the title of this chapter to ring in your head like a melody because humility is probably the most important trait you need to live a life like Christ.

Going into the text, Jesus is baptized by John the Baptist. It's pretty straightforward. Jesus asks John to baptize Him. John's like, "Bro, do you know who you are? You should be baptizing me."

If Jesus was a smart-aleck like I am, He would have said, "Dawg, your name is John the *Baptist.* I'm just asking you to do your job, man. Why you gotta make this into a thing?" But He didn't say that. Jesus responded, "Permit it to be so now, for thus it is fitting for us to fulfill all righteousness" (Matt. 3:15). In less eloquent terms, Jesus is saying that the baptism needed to happen in order to execute God's will. After Jesus makes this proclamation, John baptizes Him, He accepts the Holy Spirit, and God has a "proud dad" moment.

Analysis:

Jesus was a man who practiced what He preached. In Matthew 23:12, He states, "Whoever exalts himself will be humbled, and he who humbles himself will be exalted." Here we witness Jesus starting His spiritual journey by leading with humility. Being the Son of God, He had no obligation to ask John to baptize Him, which was made evident by John's reaction.

The standard Jesus set in these four short verses is one we should emulate. Not only did He walk the walk, but He also demonstrates what it truly means to be humble.

Humility is:

1. Doing the work.

Jesus didn't rest on His laurels. He could have skipped His baptism and gone straight to teaching the gospel. He didn't. He subjected Himself to the same standards as everyone else. He didn't skip steps. He put in the work. We will dig more into this in the next chapter, but ultimately, this example teaches us that faith without works is dead (James 2:14–26).

You can't take one juggling class and think you're ready to headline the circus. You have to spend months to years honing your craft. Once you put in that work, not only are you able to juggle three tennis balls, but you can also juggle three torches, two chain saws, and three axes at the same time. Your skills have grown exponentially. You can now do the basics in your sleep. All that was made possible by having the humility to realize you have to work hard for the things you want to excel at.

Jesus's baptism was His first juggling class, His first act toward preparing Himself for ministry.

If Jesus Himself wasn't above doing the work, then neither are we. There are no shortcuts to greatness. I've noticed that many people in today's time seek the path of least resistance.

They will stop pursuing certain things because it was harder than they thought it would be. To that I say, "Duh!" Any worthwhile accomplishment takes effort and perseverance. If it was easy, everyone would do it. God called you to be extraordinary, and becoming an extraordinary person requires an extraordinary work ethic, so get 'er done.

2. Not letting things go to your head.

This one is all about your mental state. When John told Jesus, "I need to be baptized by You" and Jesus had him do it anyway, it showed where Jesus's head was. He didn't allow John's comment to go to His ego. He stood on His Father's business and stayed focused on fulfilling His duty.

There are times that we reach certain levels in life and forget where we came from. We start sipping our own Kool-Aid and think we are too good for certain things. Don't get me wrong, there is nothing wrong with leveling up and enjoying the finer things in life, but don't let it to go to your head.

Where I come from, we tell people, "Keep your head on straight." As believers, "Keep your eyes on Him." Keeping your eyes on God keeps your mind in check.

When we stand in the business of our Father, we aren't focused on exalting ourselves; we are focused on uplifting His Kingdom.

3. Treating everyone with respect.

Jesus treated John with respect when He didn't have to. Let me remind you that Jesus lived during the "kiss my pinky" and "wash my feet" era. He could have *easily* taken that approach with John and come in guns-a-blazin' saying, "Bow before the Son of Man, and prepare the water so that I may be baptized" and smite John for questioning His order. He didn't do any of that. He submitted Himself to the authority that was bestowed upon John the Baptist.

The Air Force is broken up into two major rank categories: officers and enlisted. The officers outrank all enlisted personnel. That means a fresh-faced college graduate with zero operational experience can be in charge of a 20-year veteran who's gone on four tours to Iraq.

Knowing this hierarchy, officers are taught, "Respect the rank; follow the experience." That is what Jesus demonstrates here. Being the Son of God, He immediately "outranks" John, but John had the experience. John had baptized many individuals before Christ, and Jesus humbled Himself to John's pedigree.

Going back to the military, I've seen both sides of the coin. I've seen the people who follow this advice become successful because they were able to absorb and apply the wisdom and knowledge of the member with experience. I've also seen the individuals who lead with their rank struggle because they had to learn things the hard way and weren't able to garner the respect of their troops. That is why humility is important.

You have to give respect to get respect. No one likes being talked down to. No one likes feeling inferior. Don't be a person who projects those feelings onto others. Don't be a person who looks at people as less than or not worth your time. Don't mentally or physically separate yourself into a different social class. Jesus made Himself available to everyone. It didn't matter if they were a religious leader, a tax collector, or a leper. Jesus treated everyone equally and never hesitated to meet people where they were to take them where they needed to go.

Conclusion:

To close, I want to briefly cover when Jesus said "thus is fitting for us to fulfill all righteousness" (Matt. 3:15). I stated earlier that Jesus stood on His Father's business. His business was not only to die on the cross; He was also placed here to be an *example.* Think about it. If His only purpose was to die for our sins, why not sacrifice Him at birth? In fact, since God is a benevolent, all-powerful being, why does He even need to send His Son in the first place? The answer is that He doesn't.

I believe God also sent Jesus to prepare the way for the new era. The era of the Holy Spirit (Acts 1:4–8), and Jesus's life on earth demonstrated to His followers how they should live theirs. It provided us with a road map to navigate life without direct guidance from God. Furthermore, I don't find it coincidental that the first act we witness Jesus do is one that results in God's Spirit descending upon Him, so take that as you will.

What does that mean for us? Simply put, we should aspire to exemplify what right looks like. Live life as Jesus would. Even though we are all flawed individuals, our goal should be to set the best example we can and allow God's light and Spirit to shine through us.

Reflection Questions:

1. Reflect on an instance where you had to humble yourself. How did it make you feel, and how difficult was it for you to do? What lessons did you learn?

____

____

____

____

2. Are you a hard worker? Do you trust the process or look for the path of least resistance? Discuss ways you can improve your resiliency.

____

____

____

____

3. Discuss why it's important to treat everyone with respect. Why do you think social status or hierarchy causes people to look down on others? What can you do to make sure the people around you are being treated with respect and dignity?

____

____

____

____

4. Aside from dying on the cross, what other reasons do you believe God sent His Son to earth? Discuss.

____

____

____

____

5. How are you letting God's light shine through you? In what ways are you being a positive influence on others? How can you be better?

____

____

____

NOTES

CHAPTER 3
DO THE WORK

Matthew 4:1–11

Overview:
Jesus fasts for 40 days and is tempted by the devil.

Analysis:
You're probably expecting me to dive into the different ways the devil tempted Jesus and how His responses are representative of how we should deal with our own temptations. Yeah, I'm not gonna do that. In my eyes, that was the epitome of a GOAT (Greatest of All Time) moment.

When you are an all-time great, there will be moments that force you to sit there in awe and go, "That's why they're the GOAT." It's like when Michael Jordan hit the game-winner over Bryon Russell to win his sixth NBA title. Jesus going toe-to-toe with the devil and getting a flawless victory falls into that category.

I'm gonna keep it a buck. In no world could I ever see myself fasting for *40* days. I can't even work out a week straight. I also couldn't see myself coming on the other side of a 40-day fast and *not* turning that stone into a medium-rare steak and lobster with a side of pinot noir (Matt. 3:3–4). I'm sorry. I'm only human. The one thing I can say for certain is that I would not have thrown myself off the side of a building (Matt. 3:5–7).

I'm pretty confident about that one, but then again it might depend on how hungry I was and the availability of food. I digress.

So what do I want to discuss about this story? I want to talk about the importance of preparation. In the previous chapter, we saw that Jesus's journey started when He accepted God's Spirit through baptism. Now He's fasting and going through His first test of faith. I call this collective period of Jesus's life "spiritual bootcamp" because He was preparing Himself for the battles to come.

As we will soon find out, Jesus was a baaaaaad man. He was smart, smooth, and popular, and He always knew the right thing to say in every situation. People will have you think it's because He was God. I say it was because of His preparation. The difference between the two is that the first infers that Jesus was great because God is an omnipotent being who can do anything. The second is saying Jesus was great because He *worked* for it. He was great because He put in the work to be great. It didn't come by osmosis. He built Himself for the moment. He was the OG Rocky—except Jesus actually won His first fight.

The 40 days of fasting was Jesus's training montage. The temptation by the devil was Jesus getting into the ring with Apollo Creed. The angels ministering to Him afterward were His ring coaches telling Him, "You did good, champ" (Matt. 4:11). It's a truly inspiring story if you step back and look at it as Jesus, the *man*, preparing Himself to take on the world.

That is why I don't like lumping the miracles and works Jesus performed under the umbrella of "well, He's God. What do you expect?" It is dismissive of His effort and the physical and emotional pain He endured to make them happen. My man Jesus was the ultimate workhorse. He didn't skip leg day. He didn't take days off. He didn't make excuses. He got results.

I believe Jesus came to this earth on an equal playing field as everyone else. He didn't give Himself a "God advantage." He got His hands dirty and did things the hard way. The Bible states that when Jesus finished His fast, He was *hungry* (Matt. 4:2). Hunger is a human sensation. That tells me Jesus was truly a *man* while He was on earth. Two things can be true simultaneously.

It is possible for Jesus to be all God and all man at the same time. While He was in the form of man, He subjected Himself to the same temptations and trials we go through every day. What made Him special was the fact that He was able to overcome all sin through His faith and works. That is why He is the ultimate example.

Becoming the best version of yourself requires work. It requires focus. It requires deliberate dedication. Your desire to reach the goal has to be stronger than the pain you have to endure to get there. I joked about not being able to fast for 40 days, but seriously speaking, if that is what it takes to achieve what God has for you, saddle up. Lock in. Slay the beast. Do whatever you need to do to seize God's calling.

Conclusion:

The scripture glosses over the fasting portion, and I want to dive into it a little deeper before moving on to the next chapter. Fasting is one of the most powerful ways we can connect with God, and there are multiple ways to practice it.

Below describes my personal experience.

I did a no-food fast for about two weeks in 2018. It was truly the most spirit-filling experience. The biggest thing I learned is that you can't just go without food and water. You have to *commune* with God. I did so by meditating, praying, reading Scripture, and listening to gospel music nonstop.

Throughout the course of those weeks, God literally fed my spirit. I didn't feel any hunger, and I truly believed I was invincible. At one point, I had the strongest urge to pull a Forrest Gump and walk cross-country. As crazy as that sounds, I had full faith that I could do it all on God-power.

Without a doubt, fasting takes your faith to another level. I definitely recommend it with the caution of minimizing worldly interactions as much as possible. It will sever the connection instantly. I was in a fortunate position where I could focus solely on my fast with no distractions. However, the moment I shifted my focus from God to secular issues, that hunger hit me like a two-ton truck, so I would definitely suggest picking a date where you can pour maximum attention toward your spiritual growth.

Hopefully, my experience provides insight and makes fasting sound like a worthwhile endeavor. If you want to give it a try, don't hesitate to do your own research, or reach out to your pastor or chaplain for guidance. Have fun!

Reflection Questions:

1. What is something you want to be great at (spiritually or in life)? Are you putting in the reps and sets necessary to achieve greatness? Explain. How can you be better?

____

____

____

____

2. What work can you put into your spiritual life that you haven't been doing? What barriers are preventing you from doing it?

---

3. How do you view the miracles and works of Jesus? Do you see them as a God thing, or do you look at it from a human perspective (i.e., when you hear that Jesus walked on water, do you view that as a Bible story or a story about a man whose faith was so strong He could walk on water)? Discuss your thoughts on the narrative surrounding Jesus and how you believe we should view His works on earth.

---

4. Have you fasted before? How was your experience? Are you interested in fasting if you haven't done it?

---

5. Are there other things you do in place of fasting (i.e., social media detox, yoga, etc.)? How do those things make you feel spiritually?

NOTES

CHAPTER 4

POSSE UP

Matthew 4:18–22

Overview:

Jesus recruits four of His disciples.

Analysis:

I believe Jesus recruited disciples to spread His teachings once He returned to heaven. There are two lessons I pull from this viewpoint. First, knowledge isn't a monopoly. Second, surround yourself with people who believe in what you are doing, and have a desire to elevate.

Diving into lesson number one, knowledge needs to be shared. That seems like common sense, but I've witnessed individuals utilize their knowledge to become gatekeepers. They have the mentality: "If I had to struggle, so do you."

That's not how Jesus did things. Keep in mind that we just discussed how Jesus endured 40 days of fasting and temptation to prepare Himself for His ministry. He didn't make His disciples do that. He just rolled up to these dudes and asked, "You wanna follow Me?" They responded yes and posse'd up. It was that simple.

Mentorship is an undervalued and underutilized practice. When I first became an officer in the military, I was told it was *my* job to find a mentor. I never liked that mindset.

I feel as a leader we should go out of our way to provide and *offer* mentorship to others. Jesus didn't sit on a rock and wait for His disciples to find Him. He went out and found His disciples. He took them under His wing because they showed the willingness to be taught. I believe that is what we should do.

It does not take much effort to ask someone what they are working on or if they need help. It is not back-breaking to check in every few weeks or so and ask that person how they are *really* doing. If they refuse the help, that's on them, like the rich man who chose not to follow Jesus because he didn't want to give up his wealth (Matt. 19:16–22). The point is that Jesus was open and willing to offer guidance to anyone in need. Ask the question. Check in on people. It doesn't have to be your entire school or office. It could be one person. Either way, you are making a difference.

Moving to lesson number two, there's a saying that if you hang around five intelligent people, you'll be the sixth. If you hang around five millionaires, you'll be the sixth. If you hang around five idiots, you'll be the sixth, and so on and so forth. This concept was the second lesson I took from Jesus's recruitment.

Jesus recruited people who were all seeking a common goal—who were like-minded. He broke bread with sinners, but His inner circle—the people He spent the majority of His time with—were people who were aspiring to become saints. They were people who were motivated to elevate each other under the leadership of Jesus.

We must surround ourselves with people who are looking to achieve similar goals, people who have the same drive and the same work ethic. If you don't, you open yourself up to becoming the disciple Judas. The moment Judas started hanging out with the wrong crowd, he betrayed Jesus. When he realized what he had done, he hung himself (Matt. 26:14–16, 27:3–5).

The moment you start hanging out with the wrong people, you will start betraying yourself and what you stand for. I've been there. I've tried to fit in, and every time I did, I eventually fell down a path that resulted in not being able to recognize myself in the mirror. Be better than me. See the signs, and run from temptation.

No one wants to be different, but as followers of Christ, we have to be. We have to exemplify what right looks like, no matter the situation. That is a heavy and difficult burden to bear. Fortunately for us, Jesus shows us that we can share this burden when we surround ourselves with like-minded individuals. So find your crew.

Conclusion:

I will close this chapter by discussing the people Jesus decided to recruit. He didn't choose religious leaders or kings with power and influence. He chose people from humble and sometimes questionable backgrounds—people you would not expect. The key takeaway from this is that you don't have to go to divinity school to spread God's Word. You don't have to be certified to have an opinion or pursue a goal.

We live in a society that tells us we can't do x because we don't have y. Really? Did Shakespeare have an English degree when he became a playwright? Did Beethoven spend 10 years at a conservatory before he became a composer? No. They just did it.

Obviously, there are certain things that require training such as flying a plane. I want to make that clear because I don't want y'all to Key and Peele me and tell the cops, "Michael said I could fly" when they arrest you for flying a plane without a license.

The point I am making is this: don't let the world tell you what you can and can't do. Don't limit yourself. If you can dream it, you can achieve it. I have met many people who have told themselves they can't accomplish certain things because they come from a certain background, don't have a certain level of education, or are waiting for the right time. Those are all excuses. Don't be a person who looks for reasons to quit, look for reasons to continue. Don't be a person who accepts defeat the moment things get tough. Be an "I can" person.

Say "I can" get this job. "I can" pass this test. "I can" recover from this setback. Tell yourself you can do something, and then put in the work to get it done. If you approach your dreams and aspirations with an "I can" mentality, you'll be surprised at the amount of doors you'll be able to kick down.

Reflection Questions:

1. Do you have a person in your life you mentor (friend, coworker, child, etc.)? What guidance do you provide them, and how often do you interact? If you don't have a mentee, do you plan on getting one? Why or why not?

____

____

____

____

2. Evaluate the people in your inner circle. Do they motivate you to be the best version of yourself? In what ways do they have a positive impact on your life? Discuss.

____

____

____

____

3. Is there something you feel like you should be doing that you aren't doing due to an external factor (fear, doubt from others, lack of belief in yourself, etc.)? What do you think you need to do to overcome the obstacle?

____

____

____

____

____

NOTES

CHAPTER 5

KEYS TO SUCCESS

Matthew 5–7

Overview:

As you can see, this section covers three whole chapters in Matthew. Jesus gets *busy* dropping knowledge on folks—nonstop gem after gem. It hits you right in the face.

We aren't going to go into the specifics of His teachings because this book is focused on analyzing Jesus's actions. That being said, this is ironically going to be one of the shorter chapters of this book.

Analysis:

If you look at how Matthew has been laid out geographically thus far, we see Jesus accept the Holy Spirit, fast for 40 days, and recruit His team. Now He's getting to work. I interpret this as the basic structure for how we should approach pursuing our goals.

The funny thing is, many of us already follow it in some way, shape, or form. If you're a doctor, at some point in time you decided that's what you wanted to do, you went to school for it, you built a support system, and then you did the job. The only difference between what we do and what Jesus did is certainty. Jesus knew from the jump what His purpose was, and He went after it. We are often unsure, weigh multiple options, try something else for a bit, and then circle back.

I'm not saying there is anything wrong with that. I just bring it up to highlight why I believe the first seven chapters of Matthew is Jesus giving us the keys to success. I have broken it down to the following:

1. Decide what you want to do.
2. Put in the work.
3. Construct a team.
4. Do the thing.

It sounds really simple when it's laid out like that, but I think we all know that a lot of things in life are easier said than done, so don't beat yourself up if you don't "get it right" the first time around. The ultimate purpose of this list is to be a *guide* to help vector you in the right direction.

Conclusion:

Told ya it was gonna be short. The only thing I'm going to add is that this list isn't linear. You don't have to follow this exact formula step by step. It's a guide, so don't get nervous or think you're wrong if you have to go back and forth between steps.

For example, before I wrote this book, I was writing screenplays (Step 1).

I spent the next five years bouncing back and forth between putting in the work (Step 2) and doing the thing (Step 4) while attempting to construct a team (Step 3) in the screenplay world. Then I decided to write this book (back to Step 1), and now I'm jumping to doing the thing (Step 4) because putting in the work for five years with screenplays gave me the tools I needed to write this.

You got all that? I'd be impressed if you did because I wanted it to sound confusing to depict the messiness and unpredictability of life and the fact that it often comes with many twists and turns.

That's why it's important for us to ask, listen, and rely on God's guidance as we navigate through it.

Reflection Questions:

1. Where do you feel like you are in the keys to success steps? Discuss what challenges or successes you have experienced throughout your journey.

___

___

___

___

2. Which step do you believe is the most difficult to accomplish? Explain.

___

___

___

___

3. Have you ever had to start over? What made you change your plans? Discuss the challenges and benefits of starting over.

___

___

___

___

4. How good are you at relying on God to guide you along your journey? In what ways can you improve?

____

____

____

____

NOTES

CHAPTER 6

SERVICE BEFORE SELF

Matthew 8:1–17, 28–34; 9:1–8, 18–34

Overview:

Jesus heals several people and casts out demons.

I want to begin this chapter by stating that there are individuals in the 21st century with the capability of performing these acts.

However, it is not common practice by the everyday person, and this book focuses on presenting lessons any individual can learn from and apply to their lives, regardless of spiritual capabilities. That being said, this section will focus on Jesus's acts of service and how they came to pass.

Analysis:

The title of this chapter—Service before Self—is an Air Force core value, and I find it a fitting description for these sections of biblical text. The idea behind service before self is that your duty comes before your personal desires. If it's 4:00 p.m. and you still have important work to do for the mission, you stay until it gets done. Jesus was the *embodiment* of this. Jesus was never off the clock and never hesitated to assist those in need. All a person needed to do was ask and believe. It didn't matter the time of day. He was quite literally the Oprah Winfrey of serving others. "You get a healing! *You* get a healing! *Everybody gets a healing*!!"

The message we should take from this is that we can never be too busy to help those who call out for us. I think we've all had that friend or sibling who calls us at 2:00 a.m. to vent about their problems.

Let me be the first to tell you that you did the Lord's work, my friend. In all seriousness, though, it's not about us. The world may tell you to "be about your bag," "focus on you," and a plethora of other self-serving things, but that ain't from God. That's not how He expects His followers to be. He calls us to be *fishers of men*, and a part of that charge is going the extra mile to support those who need help. The only caveat is that you need to utilize discernment to determine if the person is coming from the right place when asking. For example, if a buddy of yours has a gambling problem and asks you for $20, you are not obligated to help him if you discern he hasn't repented and turned away from that vice.

The one thing I noticed with all the people Jesus healed is that they all had pure intentions in their hearts, exemplified humility, and had unshakable faith. You can't help someone who doesn't want to help themselves. You can't help someone who chooses not to see the error of their ways. You can't help someone who doesn't believe in a brighter tomorrow. All of these are prerequisites. You'll only be able to truly help them *after* they accomplish this. Otherwise they will just be a leech sucking away all your time and energy.

Conclusion:

There will be times you might have to allow your friends to be the prodigal son and find their own way back home (Luke 15:11–32), but when they do, be ready to meet them with open arms and let them know they are loved unconditionally.

Furthermore, I can't end a chapter about being there for people without acknowledging that we live in a cut-people-off and block-them generation. Here are my thoughts on that. There are some people who are brought into our lives for a season. Everyone isn't meant to be a lifelong friend. I also believe that people can do things that put us in a position where we need to pull away. It happens. However, we still need to be available.

When I say "available," I mean strictly in an assistance capacity. That's it. You are in no way obligated to rebuild a personal relationship with that person.

As an adult, Jesus only had a close, personal relationship with 12 people on a day-to-day basis. He helped thousands, but the only consistent individuals in His life were His disciples. If Jesus kept His inner circle small, you shouldn't feel pressure to make every person you meet your friend.

Finally, there will be some individuals who manipulate your kindness to weasel their way back into your life. That is where discernment and prayer come into play. Always do a quick check-in with the Big Man upstairs when you aren't sure how to handle a situation.

All in all, it may be difficult and for some impossible, but to live a life like Christ, we need to push aside our personal feelings and do what Jesus would do.

Reflection Questions:

1. Are you a dependable person? Do you make yourself readily available to others?

2. Have you ever let a friend or loved one learn a lesson the hard way? What happened, and how difficult was it to allow them to figure it out on their own?

3. Have you ever cut someone off? If so, how would you feel and react if they came to you in a time of need? Would you be able to push aside your feelings to help them out? Why or why not?

NOTES

CHAPTER 7

SAY IT WITH YOUR CHEST

Matthew 9:1–17

Overview:

This chapter is a crash course on how to deal with haters—back-to-back-to-back stories of people challenging and questioning how Jesus operated. My personal favorite was when they asked Jesus why He was hanging out with the tax collectors and sinners. Jesus responded, "Those who are well have no need of a physician, but those who are sick" (Matt. 9:12). BOOM! Mic drop! That was by far one of the *coldest* comebacks I've read in the Bible, and Jesus came up with it off the dome.

The analysis of this chapter will highlight the following from the three encounters: (1) the lessons to be drawn from each, (2) the people involved, and (3) the power of speaking from purpose.

Analysis:

Lessons:

1. The first story involves Jesus forgiving a paralytic for his sins. A few scribes say within themselves, "This man blasphemes." Jesus senses their thoughts, claps back at them, heals the paralytic, and leaves the crowd speechless (Matt. 9:1–8).

Aside from this being one of the first instances we see Jesus being a straight boss, it is worth emphasizing that Jesus responded to what was in these men's hearts, not what they actually said.

The lesson to be taken from this is that there will be people you meet who prey on your downfall—people who smile in your face but hate you in their hearts, people who judge every step you take. This judgment can come in many forms. It can be a snide remark, a disapproving glare, talking smack behind your back, you name it.

Regardless of the tactic, you can't allow their negativity to stop you from fulfilling your purpose. You can't operate from a mindset that is overly concerned about other people's opinions about you. It clouds your decision-making. I've often seen it paralyze people and prevent them from moving forward in their journey because they develop anxiety from constantly thinking about everybody's perception of them. They'd rather do nothing than have to deal with the emotional toll of criticism. You have to block that out.

To be clear, I'm not suggesting that you become an emotionless rock. God gave us feelings for a reason. I'm saying that your purpose has to be greater than their persecution. It's okay to have things affect you, but you can't be affected. It can bother you that none of your coworkers like you, but you still have to do your job.

You can't allow your feelings to affect your mission. You might need some time to recover from the emotional blow, but you must keep going. Jesus took His criticism in stride. To save face with the scribes, He could have responded, "My bad. I meant to say *God* forgives him of his sins. Not me." He didn't do that. He said, "Why do you think evil in your hearts . . . the Son of Man has power on earth to forgive sins," and then He went back to finishing His business (Matthew 9:4–5). He didn't back away from adversity. He doubled-down. He took it head on and spoke with conviction.

2. The second story was outlined in the overview. It's Jesus maxing and relaxing with a bunch of sinners (Matt. 9:9–13). The lesson here is pretty simple: *branch out!* Stop staying in your comfort circle of people who think, talk, and act like you. Those aren't the people who need your guidance and light. They get that on a regular basis. Talk to a stranger. No one is asking or expecting you to become best friends. Just have a conversation. A few minutes of your time can go a long way for someone else, but I will reiterate: friendship is *not* required.

Jesus hung out with these people once, and we never heard from them again. Matthew the tax collector joined *Him*—not the other way around (Matt. 9:9). I believe this whole situation was intentional. You've probably heard the phrase "bad company corrupts good character." Connecting this saying back to the "Posse Up" chapter, if you hang out with five sinners, you'll become the sixth.

Keep this in mind as you start branching out. That is why you don't want to spend obscene amounts of time with people who are still lost and finding their way. The intention is to make a positive impact by showing God's light and love. If they want to come along for the ride, great. If not, go on about your business.

Finally, nurture the potential you see in others. The Bible doesn't dive into why Jesus recruited Matthew as a disciple, but for context, tax collectors were not good dudes. They were dishonest thieves who were hated by pretty much everyone.

For Jesus to choose someone with this background to become His follower means He saw something in him that no one else did. He believed in what Matthew could become and took him under His wing to help him soar.

If there is someone in your life who you believe has potential, take them under your wing. Help them see the things you see, and guide them until it becomes a reality.

3. In the third story, the followers of John the Baptist and the Pharisees ask Jesus why they have to fast and Jesus's disciples do not. Jesus tells them that the point of fasting is to connect and be closer to God, and the disciples didn't need to do that because they spent every day with Him (Matt. 9:14–17). That teaches us to be intentional with our actions. Understand why we do the things we do, and ensure that our actions have meaning behind them.

Don't be a person who takes communion on the first Sunday of the month because everyone in the congregation is doing it. Do it in remembrance of Jesus. If you're only doing it to follow the crowd or because it's what you are supposed to do to be a good Christian, then it's an empty gesture with no meaning.

It's like when a celebrity issues a forced apology. They aren't *really* sorry for what they did or understand why they should feel sorry; they are just going through the motions to salvage their reputation. That might work in the public eye, but we worship a God who examines our hearts, a God who isn't impressed with the dog-and-pony show. He is a God who wants true followers who have a heart for Him. Don't look the part; be the part.

Who the occurrences happened with:

In children's church, you were probably taught that the Pharisees and Sadducees were the bad guys in the story of Jesus. That isn't true. They were actually the religious leaders of the era. They were the people who told you what you can and can't do as a believer and held you accountable when you didn't follow the rules. They were . . . the church.

Now that last sentence is gonna get me in trouble, but it's true. The Pharisees and Sadducees were the established order. Jesus was the rebel, the troublemaker, the "bad guy" by their standards. Jesus even says as much in the next chapter of Matthew.

> Do not think that I came to bring peace on earth. I did not come to bring peace but a sword. For I have come to "set man against his father, a daughter against her mother" . . . . And he who does not take his cross and follow Me is not worthy of Me. He who finds his life will lose it, and he who loses his life for My sake will find it.
>
> —Matt. 10:34–39

I told you that Jesus was a baaaaaad man. He did not come to play. He came to spark a spiritual revolution and change the long-held beliefs of the church.

To clarify, when I say "the church," I mean religious institutions that rigidly follow traditions over truth—the institutions that believe if you follow certain principles and practices, that makes you a good believer, and if you don't, you are going to hell. The truth is that we are all sinners who are worthy of hell, but through the grace of God, we are granted eternal life with Him (Eph. 2:8–10, Rom. 3:10–26, Rom. 6:23).

So if you are part of a religious institution that discriminates based on race, sexual orientation, criminal or drug history, gender identity, or honestly anything, you are part of what I call the Pharisee/Sadducee cult. You are part of an institution that believes they are superior to others because they "got it right" in the practicing religion category.

It is truly saddening because these institutions don't follow what I believe to be the most important verse in the Bible—"He who does not love does not know God, for God is love" (1 John 4:8).

It's written as clear as day and is honestly our only job to our fellow man. Love one another. Love the sinner; hate the sin. Treat everyone with respect and dignity regardless of differences.

Before moving on, it's important to note that you don't have to condone every action a person does in order to love them. Love is also accountability. It's *educating* someone on what's right and wrong according to biblical principles when the opportunity presents itself.

The reason I put an emphasis on educate is because it isn't your place to pass judgment or condemnation on someone else when you have your own issues to worry about (Matt. 7:1–5). We are all a mess, and the best way to clean up a mess is by pitching in and helping—not condemning. Follow the golden rule—do unto others as you would have them do unto you. It will help keep you in check on how you treat people who are different from you.

Speaking from Purpose:

The final thing I am going to touch on before closing this chapter is the power of speaking from purpose. This is a phrase

I created that means talking on behalf of something greater than yourself. When Jesus clapped back at the religious leaders, He wasn't doing it to defend Himself. He was doing it to glorify His Father and justify helping others. It wasn't about Him.

You've probably noticed that when people talk crazy to you, you tend to tolerate a lot more than when they talk crazy about someone you care about. There's a ferociousness that emerges when you see someone you love being taken advantage of or belittled, and when you speak up for them, there is strong conviction. That is speaking from purpose. In that moment, your purpose is to protect the individual and let their attacker know they are not alone.

The power comes from taking yourself out of the equation, focusing on the greater good, and doing right because it's the right thing to do. It's focusing on bringing glory to God through your actions and knowing that through Him all things are possible (Phil. 4:13).

Conclusion:

When speaking with purpose, say it with your chest. Jesus *never* minces words or stutters when He's schooling someone both literally and figuratively. This is the example we should strive to emulate because confidence affects competence.

If you don't sound like you know what you are talking about, people won't believe you know what you're talking about. You can't effectively defend a person or principle from a place of self-doubt or meekness. You have to be ferocious. People need to feel like you mean business. They need to feel like you are a bad mutha hush yo mouth. Otherwise, your message can fall flat, be ignored, or give the impression that you are a person who can be manipulated. Say it loud! Say it proud!!

Reflection Questions:

1. How much do other people's opinions matter to you? Does it make you feel self-conscious? Discouraged? Does it affect your mood? Why do you think you place so much value on other people's perceptions, and what can you do to lessen the effect they have on you?

____

____

____

____

2. When is the last time you had a conversation with a stranger? How did it go? After reading this chapter, do you feel like you should branch out of your social circle more? Why do you think it's important to meet new people?

____

____

____

____

3. Do you feel like you are going through the motions for things that should be done with intention (i.e., sports practice, prayer, your job)? What can you do to ensure that you are accomplishing these actions with the intentionality they deserve?

____

____

____

____

4. In your eyes, who are modern-day Pharisees and Sadducees? Why do you feel this way? Are there things you do in your personal life that mirror their mindset? What are you going to do to overcome these prejudices or biases?

5. Reflect on a time you spoke from purpose. Why did you do it, and how did it feel?

NOTES

CHAPTER 8

LEAVE A LEGACY

Matthew 10

Overview:

Jesus gives His 12 disciples the power to heal and cast out demons, and then He sends them out to preach the gospel. He also warns them of all the things to expect during their journey and how to respond to persecution.

Analysis:

This is the final step in living a life with purpose—leaving a legacy.

Jesus led by example and showed His disciples His vision. Not only did He teach the gospel, but He also made a difference. He changed lives. After demonstrating who He was and what He valued, He empowered His disciples to do it themselves. Before He sent them on their way, He prepared them for the adversities they would face along their journey. Kinda gives you a "circle of life" feeling, doesn't it?

The only difference is that Jesus wasn't anywhere near done. He was just getting started, but He knew that the best way to leave a legacy was to have His successors grow with Him. That is the exact *opposite* of what we were taught in movies such as *The Karate Kid*, *Kung Fu Panda*, and *Willy Wonka & the Chocolate Factory.*

Almost any movie about choosing and training a successor is about some older guy who is well past his prime giving the young guy some sort of test to show that he's worthy. It's great for cinema but bad for real life. Jesus shows us that we don't need to be special to do something special. Need I remind you that a third of Jesus's posse fished for a living? They were not the most qualified individuals.

In the "Posse Up" chapter, I talked about mentorship and how we should seek people to mentor and not wait for someone to beg us like LaRusso did with Mr. Miyagi. Jesus sought out people to teach, and so should we. Pick someone, and be the mentor you wish you had. Once you have shown them the way, give them the space to do it on their own.

I've noticed that just like the movies I listed, we like to offer guidance when we have one foot out the door. "This is my last week here, so now I'm going to tell you all the ins and outs of the workplace." Don't be like that. Help people while you're in a position to help and course-correct.

I believe there are two major barriers that prevent us from being actively involved in the development of others. (1) We are so focused on achieving our personal goals that we don't even think about doing it. (2) We don't think we have enough experience to provide guidance of value.

As a person who is goal-driven, I definitely fit into barrier number one. I often get so wrapped up in the things I have to do to achieve my dreams that I don't even think to take anyone else along for the ride. The thing that has helped me become a better mentor is constantly thinking about what I wish I had known when I first started and sharing that information with the new people coming in. Focusing on making sure everyone in the office is set up for success made it much easier to go out of my way to provide insight to the people I was teaching.

For the second barrier, I'm going to ask you a question. If a friend came to you and asked if a movie you just watched is any good, you'd confidently state your opinion and go into the different elements that made it a good or bad film, right? Of course. We've all done it. Most of us are not qualified to feel the ways we do since we aren't filmmakers, directors, or cinematographers, but we do it anyway. Why? Because deep down we want to help people. We want to give people insight that allows them to make the most informed decisions.

We need to keep that same energy toward mentorship. You may be afraid to say something stupid or wrong, but some advice is better than no advice, and both you and that individual will learn and grow from the experience. Shoot your shot.

Conclusion:

I'm a huge sports fan, and one of the things I've observed recently is that people devalue others' opinions based on the resume of the person they are talking to or about.

They say things like, "You can't say this player is bad because they are better than you," or "What have you proven that entitles you to feel the ways you do?" That attitude is ridiculous. As mentioned previously, we *constantly* give our thoughts and feelings on things we have *zero* qualification for.

Just the other day I told someone that if they were looking for a reliable vehicle that lasts a long time, they should buy a Toyota. I'm not a mechanic. I don't know or care about the inner mechanisms of a car that objectively makes it a good or bad vehicle. I only know my experience as a customer who has owned a Toyota for half a decade.

The point I am making is to stop allowing others to tell you what you can or can't talk about. Having conversations and differences of opinions is what helps us grow and learn.

In the military, there are certain off-limit conversations such as religion and politics that we are told to avoid because they can be divisive and make others uncomfortable. My question is this: Why? Why do we as a society tell people to avoid conversations instead of teaching them to respect differences? You can't make someone believe the things you do, so why do we get bent out of shape and angry when they don't?

We need to start training our reactions to be similar to when someone tells you their favorite color is blue, and yours is orange.

You clearly disagree, but you don't hate or judge them for it. This is how we *should* react when people tell us they are pro-abortion, atheist, transgender, or whatever else is a hot topic for debate because at the end of the day, all sin is sin in God's eyes (James 2:8–13). The same holy water you want to pour on someone who is gay is the same water you should be pouring on yourself for lying to your boss about being sick so you can get a day off.

It is completely baffling how emotionally invested we get in other people's lives. God gave us free will, and it's not my or your job to impose our will on others. The only thing we can do is share a perspective, and in all my years on this earth, I have found that the best way for someone to accept *your* perspective is if they feel respected for *theirs*.

Stop trying to be God in other people's lives. Be a guide. Show them what you believe to be right, and allow them to make their own choices from the discussion. That is the most effective way to mentor. Jesus said that those who *receive* Him will be rewarded—not those who have been forced (Matt. 10:40–42).

The reason I'm harping so much on this point is because judgment and hatred hamper our ability to leave a legacy. Who is going to be open to the information you have to offer if they feel judged for their life decisions or feel like you are prejudiced toward them?

Whether you know it or not, people are watching how you treat and interact with others, and that can affect their openness with you and your ability to connect with them. Do your best to live a life free of biases because bias can turn a positive legacy into a negative one faster than you know.

Reflection Questions:

1. What do you believe is your current legacy? Who does it impact? List ways you can grow as a mentor.

____

____

____

____

2. What do you believe are your own personal barriers to being a mentor to someone else? What are ways you can overcome them?

____

____

____

____

____

3. What controversial topics are emotional triggers for you? Why do they cause a strong visceral reaction? Do you feel it prevents you from having engaging conversations about the topic? Why or why not?

____

____

____

____

4. What are your off-limit conversations? Discuss.

____

____

____

____

NOTES

CHAPTER 9

LET 'EM KNOW WHAT'S UP

Matthew 11:20–24

Overview:

Jesus warns multiple cities what future will befall them if they continue down their path of sin.

Analysis:

I love how this chapter comes immediately after we discussed how it's not our job to impose our will on others because that is exactly the example Jesus sets here. He's not forcing anyone to do anything. He's just letting them know what's up. He's letting them know that if they continue to sin, it is not going to end well for them, and then He justified His claim with Scripture.

The lesson here is that there is nothing wrong with telling someone they are headed down the wrong path. It is actually one of the strongest forms of love because telling someone they're wrong and holding people accountable is really hard to do. It's awkward and uncomfortable, and often results in arguments.

That being said, it's important for us to do it tactfully. Jesus can be blunt because He was blameless and lived by example. We, on the other hand, are imperfect people pointing out imperfections in others. We have to do it in a fashion that doesn't come off as judgmental. Otherwise, it could turn that person off to what you have to say, or they'll retaliate by calling out the things you've been doing wrong. Knowing this, I've provided a few ways to approach uncomfortable conversations.

1. Bring it up if the conversation *naturally* leads you there. I'm a firm believer that if it is meant for you to address, God will provide the opening. You don't have to force it. The only times I would force an interaction is if the person's actions directly impact someone else or could result in imminent harm to that individual (e.g., suicide).

The former is what occurs in the biblical text we are covering in this chapter. The sinful behaviors of the citizens had the potential to spread like wildfire, so Jesus initiated the interaction before it could affect more people.

The latter is more of a see-something-say-something mindset. If you know that a friend just lost a loved one and they've started drinking heavily to numb the pain, get involved. Those situations are relatively easy to point out because you are addressing an obvious change in behavior, and the intent is more so to check on their well-being than to call them out for something wrong they are doing.

2. Show your work. Don't express your feelings without qualifying it with Scripture or a personal story. Jesus didn't say, "Y'all messing up" and dip. He gave them a context to pull from. He compared their actions to the wicked city of Sodom that God destroyed in the Old Testament (Gen. 19:1–29). That

helped them understand how bad their actions were and gave them the opportunity to decide whether or not they were going to change.

If you think it's a bad idea for your friend to go to a party, don't say, "I wouldn't go to that party if I were you; they act wild over there." Say, "Hey, last year I went to a party in that neighborhood, and the cops had to break it up because someone pulled out a gun. So I'd be careful if you plan to go." The difference between the two statements is that the second one explains why you feel the way you do while also letting the person know it is still their choice to decide if they want to go.

The key word in both examples is *choice*. You have to give people the opportunity to choose what they want to do with their lives. Nobody likes being told they *can't* do something. It only makes us want to do it more. The reason we want to push the red button or touch the hot stove is not because we have an innate urge to touch red things. It's because someone told us not to. That's how Eve was tempted to eat the forbidden fruit. The devil made her aware that it was the only fruit in the garden they weren't allowed to eat, and it enticed her to want to eat it (Gen. 3:1–7).

Conclusion:

When addressing sensitive topics, we must take into account human nature. If a person feels judged, they are less receptive to what you have to say. If they feel like you are telling them *not* to do something, the more they will want to do it.

You also have to pick the right time and place. A person needs to be in the right frame of mind to have serious conversations.

Telling someone that their pet died right after they just found out they got hired at their dream job may not be the best move. Use discernment and good judgment to feel out when and where is appropriate. A good rule of thumb to follow is if it doesn't feel right, then it isn't right. If you wouldn't want someone talking to you about a serious topic at that place and time, then don't do it to someone else.

Reflection Questions:

1. Reflect on a time you had to have a tough conversation. How did it go, and were they receptive to what you had to say?

____

____

____

____

2. List ways you approach tough conversations. What have you found to be the most effective?

____

____

____

____

3. Is there a conversation you feel like you should be having that you are holding off? What is keeping you from addressing the issue?

____

____

____

____

____

4. Reflect on a time you had a tough conversation that *didn't* go well. What went wrong, and what could you have done better?

____

____

____

____

____

NOTES

CHAPTER 10

HATERS GONNA HATE

Matthew 12:1–14

Overview:

Jesus and His disciples go against the rules of the Sabbath. The Pharisees question them and then begin plotting Jesus's downfall.

This lesson is going to be really short because we talked in depth about the ways the religious leaders treated Jesus in "Say It with Your Chest", and we will continue to talk more about them in the chapters to come.

Analysis:

Haters gonna hate. You can't avoid it. You ain't living a life like Christ if you don't have haters. Wherever there is good, right around the corner is someone waiting to wipe that smile off your face. You have to be strong. You have to be vigilant. You have to take that negativity as a sign that you are doing something right and keep trudging forward.

The sad reality is that the people who are supposed to love you the most might be your biggest haters. Look at Jesus. The majority of the hate He received during His ministry came from the religious leaders. The people who were supposed to be on His team were the ones who had the most negative things to say. They were the ones who had Him crucified (Matt. 26:1–5).

The problem was that they were driven by self-righteousness and not God's righteousness. They envied Jesus and His influence. They hated how He did things outside of their customs. They had a spiritual superiority complex that drove them to give Jesus grief every chance they got. This is the war we sign up for as followers of Christ. Not only do we have to battle the enemy, but there will also be times we have to battle the home front—the people who are supposed to have our backs.

Jesus's entire ministry is a master class on how to manage home-front haters. The religious leaders constantly questioned Jesus's actions, yet He persisted. He never let their negativity drive Him away from glorifying His Father through His works. If your actions are glorifying and uplifting to the Kingdom, let them be mad. Never feel guilty or wrong for spreading joy and positivity in the world. Never allow people to make you feel bad for blessing others with what you've been blessed with.

Conclusion:

In 2018, someone put my phone number on a Craigslist ad, and I received over a hundred texts from strangers asking if my loveseat was still available. Instead of getting annoyed, I decided to use it as an opportunity to allow God's light to shine through me. I responded to all the texts saying that it was a wrong number, and then told them that Jesus loved them and if they needed prayer over anything, just ask. The majority said thanks, and a few asked me to pray for them. Overall, it was a pleasant experience . . . until *Dave* texted me.

Now I don't remember if his name was Dave, but for dramatic effect, I think the story reads better if my hater has a name. Anyway, Dave texted me back and said, "You shouldn't be sending texts like this to people because you're forcing your beliefs on them. Just say wrong number, and leave us alone." I found what he said quite rude. Not only did I find it rude, but it also made me question if he was right. Was I being extra? In that moment I realized the power of negativity. I received a hundred positive responses to my text, but one hater made me question whether or not I was doing the right thing.

We live in a world where a hundred people can tell us we are beautiful, talented, smart, or inspirational, but if one person tells us we aren't, that's what we hold onto. That's what speaks the loudest to our self-worth. We have to recognize and accept this because there will be times we are headed down the right path, and someone will say something that sows doubt in our minds.

Don't . . . let . . . them . . . win! Your voice is powerful. Your presence is inspirational because you are created in God's image, and God don't make junk. Own it, and don't let haters knock you off your path.

Reflection Questions:

1. Who are your haters? How have they impacted your life?

____

____

____

____

2. Reflect on a time someone's negativity made you doubt yourself. How did you react? How could you have handled it better?

____

____

____

____

3. How difficult is it for you to maintain positivity when faced with negative energy? What are ways you mitigate the effects it has on your spirit?

____

____

____

____

4. Have you ever dealt with home-front haters (people who are supposed to have your back but give you the most grief)? What was that experience like, and how did you handle it?

____

____

____

____

NOTES

CHAPTER 11

OPERATE IN THE SHADOWS

Matthew 12:15–21

Overview:

Jesus heals a multitude of people and instructs them not to make a big deal about it.

Analysis:

Jesus teaches that when you do a charitable deed, don't let your left hand know what your right hand is doing, and if you are a person who seeks praise from people, you are robbing yourself of God's reward (Matt. 6:1–4). Operate in the shadows. Do things for the sake of glorifying the Kingdom, not exalting yourself.

We live in an era where we publicize everything we do. If we go to the gym, we post a video or picture with the caption "On my grind" or "#Progress." If we go to a fancy restaurant, we post a picture of our food because the "camera eats first." In itself, I don't see anything wrong with doing these things if your *intention* is in the right place.

If you're posting it to inspire or motivate others to match your energy, that's fine. If you do it to hold yourself accountable to your goals, I have no complaints. I'm even good with doing it just to show people what you've been up to or have accomplished. You're allowed to be proud of yourself and share your wins with the people you care about.

It's when you do things like this for engagement, notoriety, vanity, boasting, or showing off that I start to have issues. Essentially, if you're posting these things to figuratively or literally flex to your followers, I get mad. We talked in the opening chapter about social media making us feel like we aren't good enough, so why would you add fuel to that fire?

I'm not saying we need to be overly conscious about how the things we post make others feel because someone will have an issue with anything you do. I'm saying to keep your ego in check. Don't allow your ego to turn you into an attention-seeker.

Jesus was not a person who sought praise from men. He only sought glory from the Father. In this social media generation, we are constantly looking for people to validate us and praise our accomplishments. We gotta stop. I will say this one time: *You are enough!* Stop putting your self-worth into how many likes your photo gets. Stop traumatizing your kids by dressing up as the Grinch and scaring them during the family Christmas photo to get views. I believe our desire to be noticed, to get paid, to go viral, to be seen as "someone" in the eyes of the people we interact with on these apps fuels our ego to push out this content. Control your ego. Don't let your ego control you.

Conclusion:

This chapter focused heavily on social media because I feel this is the most relevant topic for today's society. However, this lesson applies to real-world interactions as well. The one thing I would add to help you avoid being a "look-at-me" person in your everyday life is to utilize Jesus's teaching of not letting your left hand know what your right hand is doing as a Golden Rule of Humility. If you ask yourself, "Am I saying or doing this with the goal of receiving praise?" before you commit to an action, that will be an excellent way to modulate your motives.

Reflection Questions:

1. When you do good deeds, do you tell people about it or move in silence? Why?

____

____

____

____

2. What type of content do you post on your social media? Why do you post it? Do you think your posts send a positive message?

____

____

____

____

3. Are there any other areas or activities in your life where you seek validation? Why do you desire it?

____

____

____

____

____

4. Why do you think we care so much about being validated by others?

5. How good are you at following the Golden Rule of Humility? Do you find it challenging to keep your good deeds to yourself?

NOTES

CHAPTER 12

KISS

Matthew 13:1–52

Overview:

Jesus starts teaching people through parables.

Analysis:

A parable is a short, simple story with an underlying message. For example, the "Tortoise and the Hare" is a story about a tortoise beating a hare in a race after the hare decides to take a nap before crossing the finish line. An underlying message from this can be to run your race and never quit. Even if it feels like all is lost, keep chugging along, and you might do the impossible. This was how Jesus taught. The disciples asked Him why He chose to speak in parables, and Jesus responded that it helps people understand His teachings (Matt. 13:10–13).

This is a lesson in meeting people where they are. When we teach, we need to present the lesson in a way that is understandable and digestible to the recipients of that message. Don't talk over people's heads. Keep it super simple.

You also have to know your audience. You aren't going to explain investing to a 20-year-old the same way you would explain it to a seven-year-old. With a 20-year-old, you would probably go more into the technical details of bear and bull markets, mutual funds, trading options, and averaging down. With the seven-year-old, you would probably take the *Schoolhouse Rock* approach and tell them to buy low and sell high—the basics.

Either way, the message you are sending is that investing is a viable way to make your money grow.

Being able to modulate how you talk to someone based on their current level of understanding is a vital skill. It's how we connect. A brand spankin' new Christian may not be ready to talk about all the sins that will keep them out of heaven. They might need to start with foundational Bible stories and why they should pray and read God's Word. This is why it's important for you to ask what level of understanding a person has and not assume a person's background.

The reason I say that *you* need to ask is because I'm sure we've all gone through an experience where someone talked to us about something we were unfamiliar with. Instead of saying "Yo, can you explain that to me real quick?" we just nod our head and tell them, "Yeah, yeah, yeah. I know what you're talking about," while having absolutely no idea what they're talking about. We do it because we don't want to feel stupid. We don't want to look incompetent. Knowing this, we have to ensure we are creating environments that make people feel comfortable being out of the know so we can bring them in.

When I attended my first operations briefing in the military, everyone who briefed used terms and acronyms I had never heard before, and I was completely lost. I left that briefing feeling stupider than when I walked in. You don't want the people you are teaching to feel that way. It could discourage them from continuing their journey.

Take the time to ask what they have been exposed to so you can talk on that level. The goal is not to show how much you know and what they don't know, but to teach them and guide them as they navigate to their destination.

Conclusion:

You don't have to use eloquent Shakespearean words to communicate with people. Just talk to them in your own words. We live in a time where people respect those who are genuinely themselves more than people who look and sound the part. Capitalize on that. Take advantage of the ability to be your true, authentic self when talking to people. They will feel like you are talking *to* them and not *at* them.

When we put ourselves on pedestals and talk from the ethereal I'm-the-all-knowing-czar mountaintop, it is much harder to reach our audience. It gives people a you-are-miles-ahead-of-me-I-can-never-do-that feeling instead of a we-can-do-this-together feeling. You don't want to make people feel like what you have to share is unattainable for them. You want people to look at you and say, "I can do that too"—because they can. The Bible tells us that all things are possible through Christ (Phil. 4:13), so that is the feeling we should imprint upon the people we are guiding.

Reflection Questions:

1. What is the most effective way you have found to communicate with others? Discuss ways to improve your communication.

____

____

____

____

2. Reflect on a time someone talked over your head. How did it make you feel?

____

____

____

____

3. Reflect on a time you communicated poorly to someone. What could you have done to communicate the message better?

____

____

____

____

4. Do you find it difficult to communicate to people who aren't at your level of understanding? Why or why not? What can you do to get better at it?

____

____

____

____

NOTES

CHAPTER 13

BECOME A NEW BEAST

Matthew 13:53–58

Overview:

Jesus goes back to His home town, and the people He knew from back in the day didn't believe this was the same person they watched grow up.

Analysis:

In life, we go through stages. We mature, try new things, fail, pick ourselves back up, fail again, and reinvent ourselves into new people. Change is an inevitable and beautiful process that we should embrace. However, that doesn't mean the people who knew the old you will embrace the new person you've become. I'm sure we've all heard the phrase "I miss the old you" at least once in our lives.

I don't believe we can fault people for clinging to a past version of ourselves. Any form of change takes an adjustment period because humans at their core crave normalcy and stability. The people we need to be wary of are those who don't accept or believe in the transformation. Those are the people who try to sow doubt in your mind and discredit the work you put in by throwing your past in your face.

Going back to the text, the people of Nazareth made a point to bring up Jesus's upbringing in order to fuel their disbelief about who He had become (Matt. 13:55). That kept them from receiving the blessings Jesus had in store for them.

In the "Service before Self" chapter, we discussed how we live in a cut-people-off generation. To recap, my stance on that is to use discernment to decide who you need to distance yourself from, but be ready and willing to help them if they get their act together. This is an example of a moment when it's okay to distance yourself. You can't move into your purpose with people trying to suck you back into your past. The only reason Jesus didn't continue helping them was because they didn't believe in His growth. There are two lessons here.

1. Sometimes when we level up, we outgrow the people we grew up with. We become a new beast, and people still view us as the little kid trying to figure out the world. Hold your head up. Stick your chest out. Don't lower your crown for people who haven't found theirs, for people who view the changes God has made in your life as a *phase* because they haven't allowed God to change them. You've stepped into your golden era. Own it. Keep moving forward, and don't look back.

2. When people say they've changed, believe them until they give you a reason not to. Don't lead with doubt. Saul, a persecutor of Christians, became Paul, Jesus's biggest advocate, overnight (Acts 9). So I believe anyone

> is capable of getting their life together when the right circumstances arise. Treat people the way you want to be treated. If we are trying to make a change in our lives, we want support. How can we expect to be supported if we don't support others?

Conversely, I've also seen Peter deny Jesus three times after saying he never would. The moment ya boy felt that pressure, he pulled a Mariah Carey—"I don't know Him; Jesus who?" (Matt. 26:69–75). I bring that up to say that you never know when people really change, but keeping it a buck, it really ain't your place to judge someone's heart. That's between them and God. Paul became one of the greatest apostles in the Bible. His message impacted multitudes. None of that would have happened if the disciples had held his past against him and allowed him to get killed by the religious leaders when he first converted (Acts 9:20–25). If you can change, so can they.

Conclusion:

Keep climbing. Keep reaching new heights. Never settle. There is always work to be done within ourselves in order to become better people and better believers. If you develop a growth mindset, you will continue to evolve into a new, more complete version of yourself.

Along the way, you will be faced with people looking to tear you down and question your progress. Don't give their voices power. You can't control a person's words or actions, but you can control how it affects you. You are the person who decides whether doubt is going to cause you to stumble or be the fuel that propels you into a new stratosphere. Be bold. Be courageous. Be you.

Reflection Questions:

1. Have you experienced a spiritual glow up? How did the people in your circle respond to your maturation?

2. What are ways you maintain a growth mindset? How do you keep track of your progress?

3. Have you ever received a negative response to a change you made in your life? How did it make you feel? How did you respond?

4. Do you have an example of a time you doubted a change in someone else? How did you treat them? What could you have done to show them stronger support?

5. Why do you believe it's hard to accept when someone says they've changed?

___

___

___

___

NOTES

CHAPTER 14

ALWAYS ON PARADE

Matthew 14:1–21

Overview:

Jesus feeds 5,000 with two fish and five loaves after healing their sick for several hours. This is probably one of Jesus's most famous miracles. However, I'm not going to focus on the miracle itself but the events that led up to it.

Analysis:

This story is actually far more heartbreaking than people make it seem. For those who don't know, right before Jesus fed the 5,000, He discovered that John the Baptist had been beheaded (Matt. 14:1–12). Jesus was actually heading to a deserted place to be alone and grieve, but the multitudes found out where He was going and followed Him. Instead of telling them to leave Him alone, Jesus had compassion for them and healed their sick (Matt. 14:13–14).

Let me say that again, Jesus had just found out that His cousin, the person who baptized Him and launched His ministry, had been killed, and instead of telling the multitudes to buzz off and give Him some space to breathe, He helped them. Not only did He help them but He fed them afterward against the wishes of His disciples (Matt. 14:15). Jesus's ability to compartmentalize His emotions and tend to the needs of 5,000 people is incredible—straight GOAT behavior.

In the military, we are told that we are "always on parade," which means that whether we are in or out of uniform, we represent the Armed Forces. All of our successes and failures are directly tied to the military. If a service member gets arrested for a DUI, the first thing the headline will say is that the person is in the military or a veteran. It's the same if they volunteer for Habitat for Humanity. The branch you represent is tied to *every* action you take.

That's the burden you assume when you put on the uniform. You no longer represent yourself; you represent the collective.

Jesus represented the Father every second of every day. He assumed the burden of perfection. A part of that burden was tending to the masses even if He wasn't in the right mental space to do so. He put the Kingdom first and let God's light shine through Him even though He wasn't His best self.

This is one of the most important lessons in this book. Every time we step out into the world, we represent our faith, values, and character. We are always on parade, and even when we are feeling our worst, we are still expected to show our best.

Conclusion:

None of us are perfect. We all have our good and bad days, and there will be times that we show our worst side. That's okay. The point of this lesson is to make you aware that as a believer, you represent something bigger than yourself. It's not about you; it's about how God is working through you.

Unfortunately, many of us represent Him by name and not through our actions. I've heard countless stories of people leaving the faith because they witnessed someone wearing the uniform of a Christian but acting like a heathen. Domestic violence, committing adultery, abusing drugs and alcohol—the list goes on and on of people who claim to be Christians while openly living in sin. Again, we aren't perfect, but don't be that Christian who lives any way you want Monday through Saturday and then sing God's praises on Sunday. It's hypocritical. You can't pick and choose when you want to represent Christ. You represent Him from the moment you wake up until the moment you go to sleep.

Had Jesus copped an attitude with the multitudes, many of them might have lost faith. I don't believe our faith should be dependent on the actions of another, but the reality is that for some people it does, and we must conduct ourselves knowing our actions have the power to change perception. Be a reason that people come to the faith, not turn away from it.

Finally, I want to give a quick shout-out to our educators, at least the ones I've had the pleasure of meeting in my lifetime (including my mama who homeschooled me until the ninth grade). I can honestly say I've never seen an educator who allowed their personal life to severely impact their profession and how they interacted with their students. Many were emotionally steady from start to finish, even though I know there had to have been days they were battling their own life struggles.

This example is how we need to conduct ourselves on a day-to-day basis. Inwardly we can be at war, but outwardly we are giving it our all and showcasing our best—so never let them see you sweat.

Reflection Questions:

1. Do you allow your emotions to drive how you interact with people? How good are you at bringing out your best in situations where you are feeling your worst?

____

____

____

____

____

2. Have you ever had an experience where you treated someone poorly because you were in a bad mood? How did it make you feel afterward? Did you circle back and address it, or did you let it go? Discuss.

____

____

____

____

____

3. Reflect on a time you witnessed someone being hypocritical. How did that affect your perception of them? Do you do things in your life that can be viewed as hypocritical? Discuss.

____

____

____

____

____

4. List things you do to keep your emotions in check (e.g., breathing exercises, prayer, listening to music). What are things you feel like you should try?

____

____

____

____

____

NOTES

CHAPTER 15

GIVE IT UP TO GOD

Matthew 14:22–32

Overview:

Jesus walks on water after going to a mountaintop to pray.

This is yet another classic story that I am not going to talk about directly. I'll let your pastor tell you that you can move mountains with the faith of a mustard seed. My job is to give you a different perspective.

Analysis:

I view this chapter as part two of the previous chapter. To recap, Jesus found out that his cousin was murdered, went to be alone and grieve, and ended up healing the sick and feeding 5,000 people. This occurred right after that. Jesus is, for the second time, attempting to get some peace and quiet to deal with His grief. This time He succeeds and gets an opportunity to be alone and pray. When He comes back to the boat, the disciples see Him walking on water.

I wasn't there, but I don't think God said, "Man, I really feel bad about your cuzzo. Let me make it up to you by letting you tap dance on this here water." The feat came as a result of where Jesus was *spiritually*. That's the power of faith. When Jesus was at an emotional low point, He turned to God. He gave all His problems to the Father, and it cleansed and uplifted His Spirit. Think about it.

Can you imagine where you have to be spiritually to say, "I don't feel like waiting for the boat to come back so I'm just gonna walk to it"? And don't look at it as a "Jesus" thing because He asked Peter to come and join Him. Peter took a few steps on the water and fell in because he got scared, not because he couldn't do it (Matt. 14:28–31).

Here's the takeaway. When Jesus hits an emotional boiling point, He *always* turns to the Father. When we get emotional, we turn to our vices. We figuratively and literally "drink our problems away." It's not until we reach a low point *beneath* our low point that we call out to God to pull us out. *Go to God first!* If you give your pain to Him, He will restore your soul.

Conclusion:

It's okay to be sad. It's okay to cry. It's okay to be burned out. Living a life like Christ is not an easy journey. Don't make it harder on yourself by turning back to bad habits when things get tough. In my experience, it's a downward spiral that always leads to you eventually looking in the mirror and saying, "Who is this?" Why does this happen? Because in times of trouble we want to rely on our own strength instead realizing that our *actual* strength comes through Him who is within you.

"Trust in the Lord with all your heart, and lean not on your own understanding. In all your ways acknowledge Him, and He shall direct your paths" (Prov. 3:5–6).

Let Jesus take the wheel, y'all! ;)

Reflection Questions:

1. What are some things you fall back to in stressful and emotional times (e.g., an ex, food, drinking, etc.)? Why do you believe you turn back to these things?

2. Have you ever leaned on God during a time of great stress? How did He pull through for you?

3. Have you ever had a spiritual connection with God where you did something miraculous? How did it feel, and what did you do to get to that place?

4. What keeps you from relying on God in tough situations?

5. Reflect on a time when you went on a downward spiral. What snapped you back to reality?

____

____

____

____

____

NOTES

CHAPTER 16

BE "THE ONE"

Matthew 15:1–20

Overview:

Jesus is yet again questioned by the scribes and Pharisees. This time they're complaining about the disciples not washing their hands before they eat bread. Yes. You read that right. Apparently it was a tradition of the elders to wash their hands before eating bread, and the Pharisees were bent out of shape that the disciples didn't follow it.

If the Pharisees were grossed out and felt it was unsanitary to eat food with dirty hands, I'd understand. But this was just another instance of them calling out Jesus and His crew for not following the religious practices of the time.

Jesus responded by calling them hypocrites because they manipulated the commandments of God to suit their needs. Jesus then tells the disciples that it's not what goes into the mouth that defiles a man but what comes out of it, because what comes out of the mouth comes from the heart (Matt. 15:16–20).

The Pharisees believed that following rules and traditions made them spiritually superior, but the rules they followed were a perversion of God's Word.

Needless to say, the Pharisees did not appreciate Jesus's comments. In fact, the disciples told Jesus that the Pharisees were *offended* by His remarks. Jesus didn't care because the things He said were in support of His Father, and the things the Pharisees did brought glory upon themselves.

Analysis:

My mama always told me that if you don't stand for something, you'll fall for anything. Jesus stood on His Father's business. The Pharisees and Sadducees made numerous attempts to indoctrinate Jesus into their practices, but Jesus didn't budge. He corrected them on their flawed thinking and never wavered from what He knew to be true. He stood on His beliefs.

That is extremely difficult to do in today's society. The *herd mentality* is stronger than it's ever been. The pressure to go with the flow and accept things you know to be wrong can be suffocating. But to live a life like Christ, we have to be brave enough to be "The One."

Who is "The One"? In the 1957 film *12 Angry Men*, 12 jurors had to decide the fate of a teenager charged with murder. Eleven of the 12 said he was guilty, and one said he was not guilty. The movie chronicles the 11 versus one battle to get a unanimous decision. "The One" winds up convincing the 11 to vote not guilty with him, and—spoiler—the kid wasn't guilty. If you're salty that I just gave you the whole plot of the film, get over it. You've had 70 years to watch it (jk).

Seriously, though, imagine how difficult something like that is—being the only one who believes something, being on an island. Do you have the guts to stick to your guns, or would you cave in to the masses because it's not worth the fight? It's okay if you cave in. Be honest with yourself. Again, it is *extremely* difficult to do *anything* alone. That's why we need a village.

Jesus had no fear when going toe-to-toe with religious leaders, but even He didn't do it alone. Obviously, God the Father was with Him just like He's with each and every one of us, but Jesus also had His boys with Him. They didn't say anything, but they were there. They supported Him, believed in Him.

Think about the people who have your back—the ones in your corner. Even if they aren't there physically, they are with you in spirit, so you are never truly alone.

My family is my village. My pops served 30 years in the military. I've never been the most "military" person, so whenever I was put in a position that was challenging or required leadership, I asked myself if I was handling it in a way that would make my dad proud. That thought would center me and give me the courage to stand for things I believed were right. Who are the people in your life who give you strength and motivation?

Conclusion:

Our strength comes from God, but that doesn't mean we can't utilize the people around us to give us a boost when we need it.

As a Christian, you will be faced with instances where you have to fight 11 angry men—emphasis on *fight*. Standing for Christ is a war, and in war you have wingmen, battle buddies. Find yours, and carry them with you into the arena.

Finally, embrace the challenge. Your beliefs will offend people, especially in this era of "what I feel to be right is right"—this era that doesn't respect people who have values, that doesn't understand that it's possible to have values without devaluing someone else. The war is more treacherous than ever before. Get up for it. Be "The One."

Reflection Questions:

1. Have you ever been "The One"? How was the experience and how did it turn out?

____

____

____

____

____

2. Who is in your village? Do you carry them with you into challenging situations? If you do, discuss a situation they helped you get through and how they contributed.

____

____

____

____

____

3. Have you ever offended someone with your beliefs? How did it make you feel? Did it affect your confidence to stand on your values?

____

____

____

____

____

NOTES

CHAPTER 17

PROTECT YOUR OWN

Matthew 16:5–12

Overview:

Jesus tells His disciples to be wary of the false teachings of the Pharisees and Sadducees.

Analysis:

This section of biblical text makes me laugh because it is one of the most random lessons Jesus gives. The disciples are like, "Oh snap! We left our lunch back at the temple." Then Jesus hits them with, "You know who else eats lunch? Those Pharisees and Sadducees. But their lunch is *rotten*." It cracks me up every time. It's like that one friend who is always focused on business and can't shut it off even when you're chillin'. I can just imagine the disciples awkwardly looking at one another confused and not knowing how to respond to what Jesus said.

Jesus is known for a lot of things, but I've never heard anyone talk about how great a *friend* He was to His disciples. He was the older brother we all wish we had. He looked out for His boys and was about that action. The majority of the interactions we've discussed between the Pharisees and Sadducees occurred as a result of something the *disciples* did or didn't do, not what Jesus did, and every time, Jesus took the heat and defended them.

Here, He's protecting their souls, making sure that when they are on their own, they aren't tainted or seduced by the Pharisees' and Sadducees' teachings.

We must protect those we care about. Don't be someone who watches a person go down the wrong path. Say something, even if it might make them mad. As long as it's done out of love and from a place of care, be willing to take that shot to the chest. I promise that you will feel much worse if things go sideways and you didn't do anything to stop it.

Conclusion:

This analysis is focused on adult relationships, but it also applies to parenting. Protect your kids. There is a lot of content out there that our children can consume, and we have to make sure they aren't exposed to things that will negatively affect their spiritual development. The Bible says that if we teach a child the way they should go, they won't stray from it (Prov. 22:6). The key word is *teach*. You have to parent. You can't let a tablet, school, daycare, or whatever raise your kids. You have to do the job!

Also, stop trying to be your kid's friend. There's a reason you were given the title *parent*. There's a reason the Bible tells children to *honor* their parents (Exod. 20:12). There's a reason the Bible says that if you spare the rod, you spoil the child (Prov. 13:24). How are your kids going to grow up and respect authority if they don't grow up with an authoritative figure? Why would they respect anyone if they look at the person they are supposed to respect the most as their buddy?

Those are the things you need to think about when you decide to be the "cool parent." Cool parents tend to wind up with *Eli's boys* as children. Eli was a priest who allowed his sons, Hophni and Phinehas, to run buck-wild. They disrespected the Lord's house and were corrupt in their ways. Eli didn't say anything about it until *other* people started talking about the boys' poor behavior. As a result, Eli fell out of God's favor because he didn't restrain his kids (1 Sam. 2:12–17, 22–36; 3:13). As a parent, you are accountable for the actions of your children. They will go where you lead them, so who are you raising them to be?

Reflection Questions:

1. Who are the people you look out for? Do you hold them accountable and have their back?

____

____

____

____

____

____

2. In what ways can you be better for the people you look out for?

____

____

____

____

____

____

NOTES

CHAPTER 18

BE SPIRITUALLY PROACTIVE

Matthew 17:1–13

Overview:

Jesus is transfigured on a mountain in front of His disciples.

Analysis:

"Good, better, best. Never let it rest. 'Til your good is better and your better is best." —St. Jerome

This quote summarizes this section of biblical text. For those who are unfamiliar with the term *transfiguration*, the Oxford dictionary defines it as a "complete change of form or appearance into a more beautiful or spiritual state." Jesus had undergone another spiritual metamorphosis, this time in preparation for his death and resurrection.

The lesson here is to never stop growing. To recap, Jesus went through 40 days of spiritual boot camp to begin His ministry. You would think that alone would be enough to carry Him from start to finish, but it wasn't. He needed to undergo another spiritual transformation. If the Son of Man didn't settle, why should we? There is always another level we can ascend to.

There is always more growth and learning we can do.

That is why I don't prescribe to the I-need-to-work-on-myself mindset. We should *always* be working on ourselves. It's a continuous and never-ending process.

It may require a period of time where you need to focus solely on your growth without distractions. That's okay. However, in my experience, people tend to use this phrase when they have gone through an emotional or traumatic event and are trying to figure out why it happened. I've also seen it used when people continually don't get the results they are looking for in a particular situation. It feels like the phrase is synonymous for "I need to figure out why people hate me, why I'm single, or why I keep dating the wrong person." Whatever the reason, it's always a *reactive* response. That is why we go through so many struggles.

When we are reactionary, the intent is to fix a problem, not grow as a person. The only times we want to work on ourselves is when some external force makes us. If everything is sunshine and rainbows, we are "perfect" just the way we are. That's garbage. Nobody's perfect. There's always growth to be had and lessons to be learned from life, and we should strive to reach those heights because we *want* to, not because it's our last-ditch effort to solve a recurring issue.

If you noticed, in both instances where Jesus went through a spiritual transformation, He did it *on His own*. He didn't say, "I need to work on Myself" because He got tired of the Pharisees being jerks to Him. He went of His own volition because He knew that in order to be the man God needed Him to be for the world, He had to be the best spiritual version of Himself. He was being spiritually *proactive*.

Be proactive with your spiritual growth. Stop waiting until you are at your lowest to reach your highest. It is much cheaper to fix a car when the check engine light first comes on than waiting until the car stops working. It is less taxing on your soul when you are continually renewing your mind and spirit than waiting until a life circumstance forces you to do so.

Conclusion:

Every time Jesus underwent a spiritual transformation, God said, "This is My beloved Son in whom I am well pleased." I believe He said this because Jesus was being spiritually proactive. God was not only saying He was proud of Jesus for the actions He took, but He was also proud of the fact He took them on His own.

It's like if your kids cleaned the entire house without being told to. Yes, you'd be happy if they did it after you told them to, but there will be an extra sense of pride and appreciation if they did it on their own. That's the moment I feel God was having with Jesus here, and I believe that's the moment He will have with us when we choose to be spiritually proactive.

Reflection Questions:

1. Are you spiritually proactive or reactive? How so? In what ways can you be better at being spiritually proactive?

____

____

____

____

____

2. Reflect on a time you were spiritually reactive. What were the circumstances that led to it?

3. Why do you think it's important to be spiritually proactive?

4. Do you have a mindset of continual growth? What are the things you do to renew your spirit?

5. Why do you believe people go to God at their lowest points instead of keeping Him part of their daily lives? Discuss.

NOTES

CHAPTER 19

KNOW YOUR LIMITS

Matthew 17:14–20

Overview:

Jesus heals a young boy His disciples couldn't heal themselves. The disciples ask Jesus why they weren't able to, and He responded that it was because of their unbelief accompanied with the fact that the particular demon they were dealing with required fasting and prayer to expel.

Fun Fact: This is also when Jesus uses the phrase "faith of a mustard seed" (Matt. 17:20).

Analysis:

This story is interesting. There aren't any specifics about what the disciples tried that led to Jesus's response about their unbelief. The reason it's interesting is because this isn't the first time they've cast out demons, so it's a little confusing as to why Jesus would say anything about them having unbelief, considering they've done these types of acts before. My guess comes from examining human nature.

I imagine the disciples attempted to do what they normally did to cast out demons. It didn't work, and they started to doubt their ability to do it the more they failed. It's kinda like when you take a test and don't know the answer to the first few questions, so you start feeling like you don't know anything at all. This is the first lesson.

In life, you are going to hit snags and speed bumps. You are going to go through trials that make you question whether or not something is meant for you to do. Don't let the doubt win. If God has named it and claimed it for you, it *will* happen. It may not come when you want it, but it'll be there right on time. Trust in God's timing.

The second lesson is that there are some things in life we can't achieve with our own strength. We need a little divine intervention or someone else to create a path. That someone else is a person with more experience or pull to get things done. The reason I put this lesson in here is for those who want to do everything on their own merit—the I-don't-need-anyone-I-can-do-it-on-my-own crowd. We all need a little help from time to time, and we need to have the situational awareness to know when to call on someone else. Don't be stubborn and set on doing something *your* way. You have to know your limits and go to God when you get to a bridge you cannot cross. He will let you know the next move you need to make.

Conclusion:

I've said it once, and I'll say it every time it's applicable—it takes a village. The Bible says it's not good for man to be alone (Gen. 2:18). God puts people in our lives with varying levels of experience and talents for a reason. Don't be a person who believes you can "put the team on your back" in every situation.

We haven't gotten there yet, but even Jesus needed help from God to follow through with His crucifixion (Matt. 26:36–44). That alone should tell you that you are not meant to tackle every challenge alone and unafraid.

Finally, pray without ceasing. As mentioned in the previous chapter, people tend to go to God as a last resort when issues arise. Hopefully, by reading these chapters you will be inspired to pray, meditate, and read the Bible with more regularity because your ability to deal with life's curveballs becomes a lot easier when you have a consistent relationship with God.

Reflection Questions:

1. Have you ever felt like giving up when you hit a speed bump? Did you quit or find a way to get over the hump? Discuss.

____

____

____

____

____

2. Have you ever doubted your ability to do something? What caused it? How did you get your confidence back?

____

____

____

____

____

3. Are you a person who likes to get things accomplished on your own? Do you have trouble asking God or people for help? Discuss.

____

____

____

____

____

4. Reflect on a time you needed someone else to help you achieve a goal. How difficult was it to ask that person for help, and what did you learn from the experience?

____

____

____

____

____

NOTES

CHAPTER 20

KNOW YOUR STUFF

Matthew 19:1–12

Overview:

The Pharisees test Jesus's knowledge about divorce.

Analysis:

Look at this as a follow-up to the "Haters Gonna Hate" chapter. When someone preys on your downfall, they look for any and every opportunity to either catch you slipping or set you up to fail. That is why it's important to know your stuff.

Credibility and competency are like reputation. It takes years to build but only one slap at the Oscars to destroy. You can tell someone the correct capitals of 32 US states in a row, but if state number 33 is wrong and someone calls you out on it, the person will immediately start doubting you or hit you with the classic "Are you sure? Are you sure you're sure?" when you name the remaining 17. You know what I'm talking about. I'm sure we've all slipped up and said something incorrect and had people question if we even know what we're talking about.

It happens to everyone.

Jesus was able to skillfully pass every test the Pharisees threw at Him *and* teach them things they didn't know. They weren't able to put a blemish on His credibility. Unfortunately for us, we aren't perfect like Jesus was. We make mistakes. We misspeak. We mess up time and time again. Our enemies will have opportunities to catch us slipping and capitalize on them. It's inevitable.

The only thing we can do is be on alert for situations people can exploit and weaponize against us, and prepare for them the best we can. You never know when that time will come, but if you stay ready, you never have to get ready.

Conclusion:

Jesus demonstrates the power of knowing what you're talking about. People came from far and wide to hear His teachings because He knew His stuff, and in the process of being taught, these people were also healed and fed both spiritually and physically. That is why we need to strive to become as knowledgeable as we can on the things that are relevant to our lives. You never know when someone will come to you seeking knowledge but leave being mentored, spiritually healed, supported, or even… a friend.

Reflection Questions:

1. Reflect on a time when a hater caught you slipping. What was the fallout that resulted? Were you able to recover, and what did you learn?

____

____

____

____

2. Reflect on a time when a hater weaponized a mistake you made. What was the fallout that resulted? Were you able to recover, and what did you learn?

______

______

______

______

______

3. Are you putting in maximum effort toward being knowledgeable in your areas of expertise? Why or why not? In what ways can you be better?

______

______

______

______

______

4. Has anyone ever come to you seeking knowledge and you gave them more than they asked for (e.g., a friendly conversation about life, mentorship, a restaurant recommendation for them to take someone on a first date, etc.)? What came of it, and how did it make you feel?

______

______

______

______

______

NOTES

CHAPTER 21

MO' MONEY, MO' PROBLEMS

Matthew 19:16–24

Overview:

A rich man asks Jesus what more he has to do to get eternal life. Jesus tells him to sell his worldly possessions and follow Him. The man doesn't do it because he is unwilling to part with his possessions.

Analysis:

We all like things—clothes, cars, houses, food, you name it. There's nothing wrong with having nice things, but you can't allow your spiritual health to be affected by your wealth. The things you buy are a blessing—nothing more. If you keep that mindset, you'll be just fine.

However, we live in a world where we often tie our self worth to the things we have—a world where people crave the attention that comes with the stuff they buy, a world where people want to look the part instead of being the part. And even when we get the things we want, we still want more. It's never enough.

All of that is a byproduct of the different forms of media we consume. We see someone has a "better life" than us, and we want to emulate it or exceed it. We look at what we don't have instead of being thankful for the things we do have. We start to allow ourselves to be driven by greed. Money and nice things become the lords of our lives, and we will do anything to get the things we want.

Jesus teaches us that a man cannot serve two masters (Matt. 6:24). That tells me that contrary to popular belief, life's not about "getting the bag." You're either living life for God or living life to make a buck. There's no in-between. The Bible warns us of this. "Do not lay up for yourselves treasures on earth, where moth and rust destroy and where thieves break in and steal; but lay up for yourselves treasures in heaven. . . . For where your treasure is, there your heart will be also" (Matt. 6:19–21).

I really like the moth and rust part because it speaks to temporariness. Not only are the things we buy temporary, but so are the feelings we have when we get them. The high we get when we buy something new fades. That brand new iPhone or Tesla becomes last year's model in a year's time, and just like any other high, we can find ourselves jonesing to replicate that feeling. It can become an insatiable appetite if we allow it to control us, and the emergence of targeted ads has made it far easier for us to become materialistic.

Society preys on our desire for things and uses any avenue it can to get a sale. Companies have your favorite celebrity promote products they don't even use just to entice you to buy it—to give what they are selling the appearance of being a status symbol.

Don't fall for the trap. Again, there is nothing wrong with having "treat yourself" moments, but don't allow yourself to become a person defined by your possessions.

Don't allow your life to revolve around chasing after things you can't take with you to your grave. I've seen people go into debt trying to keep up with the latest trends, trying to keep up with a lifestyle their bank account can't maintain, and living above their means. All of that is included when we talk about money and worldly possessions being the God in your life. I'm here to tell you that literally none of it matters. It's nice to have things, but to reword a very popular saying, money can't buy salvation.

Conclusion:

I find it very intentional that Jesus taught about worldly possessions and never discussed His own. He never talked about having a nice home, buying the latest robe from Bethlehem.com, or even owning a toothbrush for that matter. None of that was important to Him. I think this example is a good test to see if we have a heart for things. The next time you buy something cool, don't tell anyone about it. Just get it and keep it to yourself. If you feel the urge to show it off, it could be a sign that you might be caught up in material things.

Finally, I believe the concept of serving two masters can extend beyond possessions. It can be work, an activity, another person, and really anything that pulls your focus away from strengthening your relationship with God or the responsibilities He has bestowed upon you (e.g., being a parent or spouse). Be on the lookout for these traps as well.

Reflection Questions:

1. How much does having nice things matter to you? Do you think it affects your relationship with God? Discuss.

2. Besides money and possessions, list other ways a person can serve two masters. Have you ever experienced or witnessed someone doing it? How could you tell?

3. What are good ways for you to test whether you are serving two masters?

4. What about society makes it the most difficult to stay focused on what's important?

NOTES

CHAPTER 22

BE COMPASSIONATE

Matthew 20:29–34

Overview:

Two blind men call out to Jesus, and He heals them out of compassion.

Analysis:

Throughout Matthew, we've witnessed Jesus healing a multitude of people, so you're probably wondering what makes this particular instance special. The reason we are taking time to discuss Jesus healing two blind men is because this is the third and final instance the book of Matthew explicitly states that Jesus committed an act after being "moved with compassion." The first two instances occurred when Jesus fed 5,000 and then 4,000 people (Matt. 14:14; 15:32). We will be diving into the unique motivations for each situation.

Feeding 5,000: This was when Jesus went to be alone after finding out that John the Baptist had been beheaded. As we discussed in the "Always on Parade" chapter, this was a period of grieving for Jesus as He mourned the loss of His cousin. I believe the emotional pain He was enduring was what drove Him to be compassionate toward the multitudes. This compassion resulted in Jesus healing their sick and feeding them.

Have you ever heard the saying "hurt people hurt people"? This is the opposite of that. Jesus was hurting, and instead of taking that hurt out on the multitudes, He healed them. He didn't pop off on them and tell them to leave Him alone. He showed them compassion. He didn't allow His emotional state to drive how He treated the innocent.

It's very easy in moments of high emotion to take our frustrations out on others. We can't hurt the people who hurt us, so we take it out on those who haven't done us wrong. Jesus is showing us that we should treat those people with compassion. Don't continue the cycle of inflicting pain. Don't yell at your child when they ask you to play with them because you're still upset about being chewed out by your boss. Make a positive impact. Show them the love and compassion that you wish was shown to you.

Feeding 4,000: Here, Jesus shows compassion after witnessing the loyalty and faith of the multitudes. They stayed with Him for three days and had nothing to eat. He gave them food so they wouldn't faint on their journey home.

The lesson I gleaned from this is to be compassionate toward the needs of others. If they invested their time toward supporting what you're trying to achieve, do right by them.

Reward their effort. For example, if you are hosting a Habitat for Humanity event and know the people working the project are going to be out in the sun for eight hours, bring them a case of cold water. Don't let them end the workday thirsty or pass out from heat stroke. Put yourself in their shoes, and provide them with the things you'd expect or need if you were in their situation.

Two blind men: This is all about showing compassion to the faithful. The two blind men called out for Jesus to have mercy on them, and bystanders told them to shut up. Instead of listening to the crowd, the two men called out to Jesus even louder, and in return, Jesus showed them compassion and gave them their sight back.

There will come a time in your life when you will become a gatekeeper for someone else. Your positional authority and experiences will be something people seek as they work to reach the levels you achieved. Show compassion to those who come to you with humility. As stated in the "Posse Up" chapter, don't become a person who believes others should go through the same struggles you did in order to achieve success. Help those who can't help themselves because "to whom much is given… much will be required" (Luke 12:48).

Compassion should be given to anyone who has the bravery to make themselves vulnerable. It takes a lot of courage, humility, and strength to ask someone for help. Recognize that, and be a beacon of light that helps them navigate through the darkness. Don't be a person who impedes their progress.

Conclusion:

There are three forms of compassion discussed in this chapter—compassion to the innocent, compassion to those in need, and compassion to the faithful. The bow that wraps all three of them together is the concept of putting the needs and feelings of others above our own.

You might feel the urge to take out your frustrations on someone else. Fight it. The pain you inflict is self-serving and won't do anything to remove the damage that was done to you. All it does is hurt the innocent.

There will be times that the daily grind of life distracts you from being compassionate toward the needs of others. It happens. When my mom used to drop me off at school, she told me to be a blessing to everyone I encountered. As an adult, I've found internalizing this mantra is a good way to keep your head in the game. Focusing on being a blessing to the people you come across will naturally lead to you becoming more sensitive to their needs.

Finally, you might have the mindset, "If I had to struggle, so do you." Purge that. The things you have achieved in life are not by your own strength but by God's strength through you. Keep the past in the past, and build toward a brighter tomorrow. Be the change you want to see in the world. You can't do that if you aren't showing others the compassion you wish was shown to you when you were figuring it out. The golden rule is "Do unto others as you would have them do unto you," not "Inflict unto others the things that were inflicted upon you." Don't have a *salty spirit* filled with bitterness, pettiness, and vengeance. Fill it with love, grace, and charity.

Reflection Questions:

1. Reflect on a time you showed compassion to someone else. Why did you do it? How did it impact the other person, and how did it make you feel?

____

____

____

____

____

2. Have you ever taken your pain out on someone else? What caused it, and how could you have handled it better?

3. How good are you at considering the needs of other? In what ways can you be better?

4. Do you harbor resentment or bitterness toward the struggles you had to overcome in order to reach where you are now? Does it affect your willingness to show compassion to those coming to you for guidance? Why? Brainstorm ways you can release the hold these feelings have on you.

NOTES

CHAPTER 23

RIGHTEOUS ANGER

Matthew 21:12–17

Overview:

Jesus flips over tables and chases away merchants who are buying and selling goods in a temple.

Analysis:

I don't know about you, but I've never met someone who politely flipped a table. Jesus was clearly *livid* when he saw what was being done in a house of worship. His reaction to the incident teaches us that acting out of anger can be an appropriate and necessary response given the proper situation.

Typically, people view anger and rage as a negative emotion because it often leads to violence and verbal abuse. The Bible even instructs us *not* to allow the sun to set on our anger or cause us to sin (Eph. 4:26–27). That is a testament to how strong and controlling anger can be and how deeply it can affect our spirit.

Here, Jesus demonstrates righteous anger. I define righteous anger as using rage in a controlled manner to drive home a point that defends a principle or person—emphasis on *controlled manner.* Even when angry, you want to maintain self control.

Don't "Hulk out" and unleash all your feelings and emotions on someone. There needs to be a specific objective or effect you are trying to achieve *through* your anger, like when a coach yells at their team during halftime. Their objective is to get the team fired up for the second half. They aren't just yelling to vent their frustrations. There is a purpose.

Jesus's anger toward the merchants was purposeful. He was driving home the point that the behaviors He witnessed will not be tolerated in the house of the Lord. Once that point was made, He went right back to healing the sick as though nothing had happened (Matt. 21:12–14). This shows that His rage was controlled and deliberate. We have to be *deliberate* with our ferocity. It has to be used as a means to meet a specific objective, and once that objective is met, we must release it. Don't carry that fire within you. Let it go.

It is also important to note that Jesus didn't react the way He did because they offended Him personally. He reacted that way because they disrespected His Father's house. What you tolerate is what you condone. If Jesus let the action pass without doing anything about it, He would have condoned it and by proxy encouraged more people to do the same thing.

All in all, the Bible teaches us that if you know what you should do and don't do it, you sin (James 4:17). So not only is it okay to pop off on someone, it can also be required of you, depending on the situation. The question is: What circumstances warrant righteous anger?

The easy answer is any actions you witness that aren't uplifting to God's Kingdom.

Bullying, physical or verbal abuse, and harassment are a few instances that come to mind. But truthfully, I believe we all inherently know what these situations are. Have you ever eavesdropped on a conversation, heard someone make a disrespectful comment to someone else, and then asked yourself if you should have said something? Yeah, you probably should have. I believe we are innately wired to protect those who can't protect themselves. We just have to follow that little voice inside of us that's telling us to act. That "voice" is God's Spirit screaming for you to do something. Listen to it.

Conclusion:

I want to highlight that this chapter is about *action* and *reaction*. If you witness someone committing an *act*, *react* to it. I'm not telling you to harass people on a self-righteous crusade. We live in a world that tolerates and tries to normalize lifestyles that are contradictory to God's Word. Don't use righteous anger as an excuse to justify bigotry. Don't go out of your way to publicly admonish someone who's just living their life.

Jesus went after the merchants because they were *actively* doing something disrespectful. He didn't yell at them for being merchants. He didn't destroy the cities we discussed in "Let 'Em Know What's Up" that were acting like the citizens of Sodom. He *warned* them of their potential fate out of *love*. If you are approaching someone who is living a different lifestyle than you, ask yourself: Am I doing it out of love for them or because I hate what they're doing? That will help you gauge where your intentions truly lie.

Reflection Questions:

1. Have you ever experienced righteous anger? What was the circumstance, and how did you handle it? Was it hard to let go of the rage when it was over?

2. Why do you think it's important to use righteous anger? List the circumstances that you believe require that type of reaction.

3. Have you ever been on the receiving end of righteous anger? What did you do, and was it effective in driving home their point?

NOTES

CHAPTER 24

DON'T LOWER YOUR CROWN FOR PEASANTS

Matthew 21:23–27

Overview:

The chief priests ask Jesus who granted Him the authority to teach the gospel. Jesus answered their question with a question about where John the Baptist's authority came from. The priests had to say, "We don't know" because if they admitted it came from heaven, they'd be questioned for not believing John the Baptist, and if they said it came from men, they would risk receiving the wrath of the multitudes who viewed John as a prophet. Since they weren't able to answer the question, Jesus gave them a biblical "Bye, Felicia" and sent them on their way.

Analysis:

There's a lot to unpack here. In "Haters Gonna Hate," we established that all good works are met with some form of negativity—someone trying to tear you down and make you question what you're doing.

Jesus was no stranger to this concept. The book of Matthew is plagued with examples of Jesus defending how He and His disciples operated. What makes this situation unique is the setting.

Typically, we see the religious leaders hating on Jesus when they witness Him or His disciples doing something outside their traditions—things that didn't align with the religious practices of the time. This is the first time they confront Him for teaching the multitudes (Matt. 21:23) and the first time they questioned His credibility.

I envision the priests being like that one house on Halloween that no one goes to because they hand out apples. They look next door and see Jesus's house lined up with children because He's handing out full-sized Twix bars. Instead of giving the kids better treats, the biblical "Karens" decide to knock on Jesus's door and chastise Him for handing out candy instead of fruit. They gave Him grief solely because He was doing things differently, and it was producing better results. They were jealous that He had a following that they wished they had, and instead of reevaluating how they did things, they tried to find fault in what Jesus was doing.

As believers, be wary of people fueled by the green-eyed monster. When you are a person driven by something bigger than yourself, there is a glow about you that makes you attractive to others. It makes people want to know more about you, hang out at your desk, grab lunch with you, and a plethora of other things. You become the flame that attracts the moths.

Your haters will see this and attempt everything possible to douse your light. Don't lower your crown for peasants. Yes, I said *peasants* because only peasants go out of their way to tear someone down who is trying to bring good into the world. The priests made numerous attempts to tear down Jesus and get Him to stoop to their level, but He didn't take the bait. He always wore His crown.

The funniest thing about this story is that the priests never said Jesus was doing or saying anything wrong. They just questioned who gave Him the authority to do the things He did. This is a telltale sign of someone who is out to get you—when people attack the messenger instead of the message, when people take shots at *you* to hide *their* insecurities, when people make things personal. The moment someone makes something personal, tune them out. Don't give their words power or influence over you. Their intentions aren't pure. They aren't looking out for you. They are looking for reasons to bury you.

Jesus provides an example for handling these types of situations. He answered their question with a question and was petty about it. "Am I doing something wrong? No? Okay then"—that type of energy. Keep it quick. Keep it short. Keep it moving. People who are willing to be confrontational like this are looking for a fight.

They are looking for a reason to spark a debate. Don't give them the satisfaction. That wastes time and energy. I promise you that by not satisfying their ego, you've won.

Feeling the need to clap back only increases the chance of falling for their trap. They are looking for you to say or do something they can use against you, and the longer you keep the conversation going, the more likely you are to give them all the ammunition they need to tarnish your name. At the end of the day, it's not about who's right or wrong; it's about who gets the story out first, and they will always paint you to be the villain when given the opportunity.

Conclusion:

This chapter applies to those who are acting in ways that are glorifying to God, not those who are being self-righteous. The difference is that one is justifiable through Scripture, and the other is based on personal opinion. Jesus stood on His Father's business every second of every day, so all His responses were justified because He was always acting on God's behalf. We don't. We have flawed judgments, beliefs, and motives. So if you are going to act like Jesus in this manner, make sure your heart is in the right place and your actions align with biblical principles.

Reflection Questions:

1. Reflect on a situation where someone questioned something positive you were doing. How did you respond? How did it make you feel?

____

____

____

____

2. When you are met with confrontation, are you a person who likes to get in debates? Have you ever been in a debate with someone and said something you shouldn't have? What caused you to go there, and do you feel you should have ended the conversation earlier?

____

____

____

____

3. Has someone questioning you ever resulted in stooping to their level? Why? How did it impact what you were trying to achieve? How would you have handled the situation differently?

____

____

____

____

4. Discuss ways haters have tried to bring you down. Were their efforts effective, or were you able to fight the urge to quit? Explain.

NOTES

CHAPTER 25

STAY ON YOUR TOES

Matthew 22:15–45

Overview:

Jesus takes on the three-headed monster. The Pharisees, Sadducees, and scribes team up to form the *Revengers* in an attempt catch Jesus slipping. Each group took turns asking Jesus questions to see if they could get Him to incriminate Himself. And when I say "took turns," these clowns literally huddled together like a football team and drew up a game plan (Matt. 22:15). Jesus schooled all of them without breaking a sweat, and they never questioned Him again.

Analysis:

Aside from this being the original Playa Haters' Ball (*Chappelle's Show*), this passage of scripture teaches us to be mindful of other people's intentions toward you. Not everyone has your best interest at heart. There are those who will be out to get you.

Matthew 24:15 explicitly states that the religious leaders "plotted how they might entangle Him in His talk." They were out for blood. Fortunately, Jesus was able to perceive their motives and call them out on it.

There are those like myself who choose to see the best in people. We believe there is good in everyone. Although this is true, we cannot allow our faith in the goodness of others to blind us from seeing reality and the snake lurking in the grass preparing to strike. We have to stay on our toes. If we don't, the enemy will come in and destroy everything it can get its hands on.

Jesus recognized the religious leaders' attempt to destroy Him and responded in ways that prevented them from achieving their goal. My takeaway from this is that you don't have to run when danger comes. You can face it head on. Jesus never tucked His tail between His legs and ran from anyone. He was fearless. He wanted all the smoke and was able to take on anyone because He was wearing the armor of God. God's Word was His sword and shield. He didn't have to fear anything because He knew He stood on the side of right.

Did you ever study for a test so hard that you knew the material backward and forward? Do you remember the confidence you had when you went into the classroom and the teacher handed you the test? Do you remember the I-got-this feeling as you answered question after question correctly? You were so confident that if someone said you were wrong, you would defend your answer without hesitation. That's the swagger Jesus had.

He didn't have to run because He was built for this moment. He studied for the test. People like to say, "I'm built different," but Jesus actually was. He stayed ready so He didn't have to get ready. He was continually with God at all times. That's different than us because our spirituality is a roller coaster. Some of us are *Sunday worshipers* where we sing God's praises on Sunday and live however we want the rest of the week. Others are *trauma worshipers* who get super close to God after going through a traumatic experience.

A handful of us are *seasonal worshipers* who alternate between periods of high and low spiritual connections with God. Very few of us are *continually* in the Spirit. That is what prevents us from performing the miracles that Jesus and His followers were able to do—a concept I call *spiritual inconsistency.*

I bring this up to say that you are more than capable of going into battle like Jesus. Just make sure you're taking Him into the arena with you. Remember, everything you say or do is for God *through* you. It's not by your own strength but by Him whose strength is within you. If you are doing things to glorify yourself or satisfy your ego, chances are you will end up looking foolish like the religious leaders. If you are doing things to glorify the Kingdom, God will show up, show out, and give you the tools you need to slay the beast.

Conclusion:

I want to touch on the idea of spiritual inconsistency. It sounds like a problem that spiritual warriors will pounce on and say, "You're right! I am spiritually inconsistent. What can I do to fix that?"

Here's my honest answer to that question. Join a monastery, convent, or move to a jungle with no Internet or cell phone capability. The unfortunate reality is that it's difficult to continually be in the Spirit when we also have to live in the world—a world where we go to work four to five days a week and talk about the j-o-b instead of G-o-d, a world where we are always connected to secular things through our phones, a world that loves binging on true crime series.

The point I am trying to make is that the only way to truly be continually connected to God is to cut off any and all distractions that take your eyes off Him. I don't know about you, but I find that about as difficult as fitting a camel through the eye of a needle (Matt. 19:24).

Fortunately, the beautiful thing about God is that He understands how difficult it is to continually reside in Him and made salvation easy for us. All we have to do is believe in His Son, and we get eternal life (John 3:16). That's it. The sad thing is that there are a lot of people who have perverted this fact by interpreting the passage to mean, "I can live any way I want as long as I believe in Jesus." I would argue that these people don't understand what is meant by the word *belief*. They take it as belief in an existence, like a child believing that the Tooth Fairy or the Easter Bunny is real. I take it to mean belief in a leader.

If you're on a sports team and believe in your coach, you buy into their philosophies and do your best to execute their vision. That doesn't mean you do everything right all the time, but it does mean you are constantly working to get better at every practice so you can be the most prepared for the game. You don't say, "I believe in you, coach," and then waltz over to the bench, tell your teammates "you got this," and watch as everyone else works hard. That's how you get kicked off the team. You have to get in the game.

The Bible is God's playbook. He left it for us so we can learn His philosophies and execute His teachings. To *earn* salvation, we need to follow and execute the teachings of Christ to the best of our abilities. That demonstrates true belief—when our actions align with the words we confess with our mouths. That is why we need to study the Bible for ourselves and reside in God as much as possible.

If you are looking for ways to increase your connection with God, try the following (in no particular order):

1. Daily devotional
2. Social media/TV fast (get off the grid)
3. Attend a religious retreat or take vacation time from work and use it to go on your own spiritual retreat
4. Block out time in your schedule for prayer and meditation
5. Start a Bible study
6. Map out a schedule to read the entire Bible in a year, and stick to it
7. Go on a traditional fast
8. Volunteer for a leadership position at church
9. Listen to sermons on your way to work
10. Start a journal that chronicles your walk with God and how He has shown up in your life

Reflection Questions:

1. Are there people in your life who you feel are out to get you? How do you know? How does it affect the way you interact with them?

___

___

___

___

2. Reflect on a time that a confrontation caught you off guard. What happened, and how did you react? Were you able to navigate the situation, or did they catch you slipping?

___

___

___

3. What type of worshiper are you (continual, Sunday, trauma, seasonal, other)? Why? List ways you can increase your connection with God.

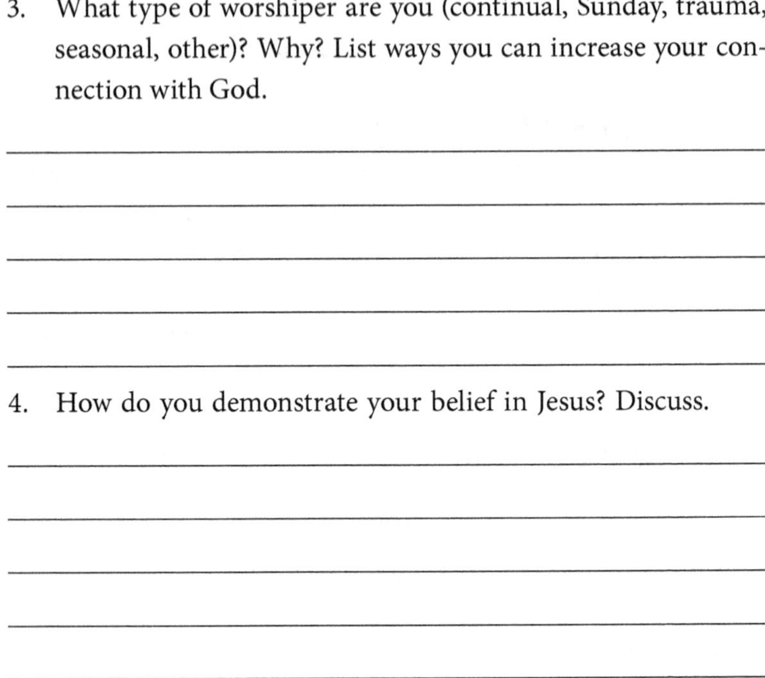

4. How do you demonstrate your belief in Jesus? Discuss.

NOTES

CHAPTER 26

BACKSTABBERS

Matthew 26:1–5, 17–25

Overview:

The religious leaders plot to kill Jesus. Later, Jesus identifies the disciple Judas as the one who is going to betray Him.

Analysis:

If Jesus, who was blameless, had to endure people scheming behind His back, we should expect the same. Will people plot to kill us? Probably not. They will, however, attempt to make you look bad at work, embarrass you, bully you, or harass you in order to meet their objectives. Be on alert.

These are the people who smile in your face and then turn around and talk smack about you as soon as you leave—the backstabbers. In boxing, they say the punch that hurts the worst is the one you don't see coming—the one that catches you by surprise. That is why it's important to use discernment when it comes to the people you interact with. Not everyone wants to be your friend.

I'm sure we've all met someone who felt "off" to us, someone we felt like we needed to keep an eye on. They didn't do anything, but something about them just makes us want to proceed with caution. Trust your instincts, and keep a watchful eye on their movements. That *gut feeling* might be God telling you this person is secretly out to get you.

You can also find yourself in a situation where a close friend switches up on you and starts acting differently. Watch out for those people as well. They might turn out to be your own personal Judas.

Yes, Judas needed to betray Jesus to fulfill prophecy, but He was still Jesus's friend and a disciple Jesus spent day and night with. Just like how we are taught to view the Pharisees and Sadducees as bad guys, we are also taught to look at Judas like a bad guy instead of who He was—Jesus's friend and follower. This *friend* that Jesus put His trust in betrayed Him for 30 pieces of silver.

Let's be real. The person who betrayed Jesus could have been anyone. Heck, it didn't have to be anyone at all. The king at the time could have ordered Jesus to be killed like King Herod ordered John the Baptist's head on a platter (Matt. 14:1–12). It didn't happen that way though. I believe God orchestrated it to go down like this to show us that anyone is capable of treachery given the right set of circumstances.

It happened to the late, great singer Selena. She was murdered by the president of her fan club—a woman who was a family friend, a woman Selena trusted enough to give a key to her house. She was considered part of the family until she got greedy and stole money from them. That got her fired. These events resulted in her taking Selena's life. Do you see the parallels?

Trusted friend—check. Greedy and selfish ambitions—check. Betrayal that leads to murder—check, check, check. There's nothing new under the sun, y'all. You can invent holograms, jet packs, and flying cars, but people will always be people. There will always be those driven by greed, lust, selfish ambitions, power, jealousy, you name it. It's up to us to sniff out the people fueled by these things and snuff it out before it snuffs us out.

Judas betrayed Jesus, but Jesus knew what was up from the beginning. He told Judas to his face that he would be the one to betray Him (Matt. 26:20–25). Despite knowing this, Jesus still fulfilled His duty and allowed Himself to be crucified.

Before ascending into heaven, Jesus left His Spirit in each of us (John 14:25–26), and I believe it is the Holy Spirit who gives us that "ick" feeling when we get around certain individuals. It's God's way of telling us that we are dealing with a wolf in sheep's clothing. Don't get fooled.

Conclusion:

Did you notice that half the attributes I listed at the end of this chapter are part of the seven deadly sins? Now you see why they're deadly. It causes people to act outside themselves. It drives them to carry out carnal, primitive urges. Protect yourself. Watch out for people who don't have your best interests at heart, and remain vigilant.

Reflection Questions:

1. Has someone ever stabbed you in the back? What happened, and were there signs they were up to no good?

____

____

____

____

2. Reflect on a time someone gave you the "ick" feeling. Did they ever do something that made you go "Yep, I knew what you were about from the beginning"? Or did you misread them? Discuss.

3. What are ways you can tell when something is off about someone? Do you trust those intuitions or wait for proof?

4. Have you ever been the victim of a scheme carried out by an enemy? What happened, and how did it affect you? Were you able to recover?

NOTES

CHAPTER 27

MIND YA BUSINESS

Matthew 26:6–13

Overview:

A woman pours expensive oil on Jesus's head. The disciples chew her out for it because the oil could have been sold for money or items to give to the poor. Jesus snaps back at them and states that her act anointed Him for His burial.

Analysis:

Jesus speaks to and influences us in different ways. One person might feel called to donate their money to charity. Another person could feel called to volunteer their time reading books at a children's hospital. It's not our place to judge how God chooses to work through others. As long as the acts are doctrinally sound, let them be, and mind ya business.

Our job isn't to be the morality police. That's Pharisee and Sadducee behavior. Where I'm from, we have a saying: Don't count other people's pockets. That means to focus on your own bank account and don't worry about someone else's. As believers, *don't count other people's blessings.* Don't look at a millionaire and tell them that they should be giving more to the community. Focus on making sure *you* are making the most of the things *you've* been blessed with.

Stay in your lane, and focus on your personal walk with God because at the end of the day, your thoughts and feelings about a person are driven by perception. And as we all know, perception and reality rarely align. So unless you're a mind reader, you don't know their true intentions. They can very well be giving back to the Kingdom through some other means. Don't make assumptions. I'm not going to spell out what happens when you assume, but I'm pretty sure that's what the disciples experienced when Jesus put them in their place. Don't let that be you.

Conclusion:

We all understand to whom much is given, much is required, but that doesn't mean we have the right to demand that others meet our expectations. Again, remember the Golden Rule. If you wouldn't want people putting their two cents in your business, don't put your two cents in theirs. We are all humans trying to navigate this circus called life the best we can. Be a person who makes that journey easier, not harder.

Reflection Questions:

1. Has someone ever judged something good you were doing or question why you weren't doing more? How did that make you feel? How did it affect your actions?

____

____

____

____

____

2. Have you ever counted someone else's blessings? What drove you to say something to that person? What was the outcome, and do you think you should have handled it differently? Discuss.

____

____

____

____

____

NOTES

CHAPTER 28

FELLOWSHIP WITH THE FAM

Matthew 26:17--30

Overview:

The Last Supper.

Analysis:

In the Christian church, we tell this story before taking communion. It's something we do in remembrance of Jesus. I also view it as a lesson about community. In Jesus's last days, He didn't spend them teaching and healing the multitudes. He spent them with His boys. That shows the importance of fellowshipping with the fam.

We live in an era where people isolate themselves from others in pursuit of a goal. They pour all their focus into achieving a dream. There's nothing wrong with aggressively pursuing your passions, but don't get lost in the sauce. Ask yourself this: When the dust settles and you've accomplished everything you set out to do, who's gonna be there with you? Who are you gonna go home to? Who are you gonna be able to share the moment with?

Jesus was the King of kings. He led *thousands* of people, but in His final days on earth, He spent it with the people who were with Him from the beginning—His A-1s since day one. That shows us how much He valued the people in His life. He could have easily spent His last days performing acts of service, but He chose to spend them with His disciples.

If He made time to commune with His family, so should we.

Quality time is a choice. Jesus was one of those people who always had something He could be doing, but He made time for the people He cared about. What's your excuse? I'll answer the question for you. There is none. There is no excuse for being an absent parent, an absent spouse, or an absent friend. It's a *choice*. Just like we choose whether or not our treasures lie on earth or in heaven, we choose whether or not we value our jobs or our family. Make it work. Some people have to try harder than others, but some effort is better than no effort.

Conclusion:

There are people in this world who don't have a support system—people who come from broken homes or estranged relationships. If you are one of those people fortunate enough to have a support system, don't take it for granted. Show up for the people who showed up for you.

If you are one of those people who don't have a support system, create one. There are many ways to create an unconventional family. Don't feel like you have to take on the world alone because life dealt you a rough hand. Find your village.

Reflection Questions:

1. Who is your fam? Do you show up for them? How can you show up for them better?

____

____

____

____

2. List ways you can show love to the ones who love you.

____

____

____

____

3. What is your biggest barrier to being there for your loved ones? Is that a personal choice or an unavoidable circumstance? If it's unavoidable, what are some creative ways you can still show them effort?

____

____

____

____

NOTES

CHAPTER 29

DON'T TALK ABOUT IT. BE ABOUT IT

Matthew 26:31–35, 69–75

Overview:

Jesus predicts that Peter will deny Him three times. Peter insists he won't, but he ends up doing it because he's scared of being identified as a follower of Jesus and being killed for it.

Analysis:

They say pressure makes diamonds, but it also makes balloons pop. The latter is what happened to poor ol' Peter. My man was talking big game to Jesus. "I would never deny you! You die, we die together!" energy. When the moment of truth arrived, Peter denied knowing Christ, not once, not twice, but *thrice*! He literally said, "I do not know the Man!" (Matt. 26:72).

If you think about it, it's kinda comical. It's like a scene from a sitcom where the lead actor is in a boxing ring about to fight someone. He's talking smack about how he's going to whoop his opponent, only to turn around and see the dude is twice his size. All his energy and bravado immediately disappear, and he starts double-talking. "You know I didn't mean none of that, right? I was just playing around. We cool, right?"

Keeping it a buck, I can't fault him for that reaction. Do you know how hard it is to not save your own skin when faced with the potential of death? Probably not. I doubt many of us have experienced a *Squid Game* situation where one wrong answer could get you killed.

I always feel like the people who roast Peter for this are the ones who watch slave movies and say, "Nuh uh! They woulda had to kill me!" Yeah, that's easy for you to say from your couch. You actually had to be there to understand what this man was going through. Cut him some slack.

Sorry for getting off topic, but I wanted to take that moment to stand up for my boy Pete because the church always gives him a bad wrap for this story. They give him the how-dare-you-deny-Jesus attitude like we don't deny Him with our actions at least 10 times a week. I digress.

Even though I empathize with Peter, he's still wrong for what he did. Obviously, he shouldn't have denied knowing Jesus, but I have a bigger issue with him saying he wouldn't deny Him and then *not* keeping his word. I'm a firm believer that our word is our bond. If I can't trust the words that come out of your mouth, I can't trust you. The Bible says it's better to not make a vow than to make a vow and not keep it (Eccles. 5:5).

The difference between a promise and a vow is like the difference between an iPhone 15 and an iPhone 15+. They are basically the same thing, but a promise is like saying, "I swear on my life," and a vow is like saying, "I swear on my mama and everything I own." It's a promise+. The way I see it, there is no difference. A promise is a promise. If you say you are going to do something, do it.

We are only as good as our word and reliability. How many times have you lost faith in someone because they weren't dependable? How many times have you stopped inviting people out because they always flake? How many times have you put the team on your back because you didn't believe your homie was gonna pull through for you? I think we've all experienced things like that to some degree. Do your best to be dependable. Don't talk about it. Be about it. Be the person you say you are, and stand up for the things you stand for.

Conclusion:

Jesus kept every promise He ever made. He was a man of His word. We should strive to be people you can count on to do the things we say we are going to do in all situations. Will there be times where "something came up" that takes precedence over the thing we said we were going to do? Yes. I'm not talking about those instances. I'm talking about when you tell your friends, "Yeah! I'll go to the gym with you tomorrow" and then don't go because you decided to sleep in.

I understand that we live in an era that wants to normalize backing out of plans, but there's a right and wrong way to do it. Don't say, "I am going to do ______" and then not do it. Say, "I might," "I'll try my best to," or "I'll think about it and let you know." That at least tells the other person there's a possibility it won't happen. Words are important and have power. If you tell your kid you are going to go to their basketball game and don't show up, do you think they're gonna care if you got swamped at work? No. All they care about is whether or not you showed up like you said you would.

Finally, don't talk a big game and not back it up. Peter became the butt of a joke, not because of what he did but because he puffed out his chest and swore up and down that he wouldn't do it. He made the situation worse by being prideful (another deadly sin).

I have a set of philosophies called "Mike's facts of life." The first one is that anyone is capable of doing anything given the right set of circumstances. You might say, "I would never get into a fight." Well, what if your sibling was getting jumped by four people and wasn't able to defend themselves? You'd probably start throwing hands to protect them. Your actions were affected by the circumstance.

Peter said he'd never deny Christ until his circumstance changed and he was literally faced with a life or death situation. The moral of the story is to be humble. Anything you can do is God-given. God is working through you for His purpose, so don't be a person who boasts about your abilities and talents because he who exalts himself will be humbled, and he who humbles himself will be exalted (Matt. 23:12). Peter exalted himself and was humbled. The same can happen to us if we aren't careful.

Reflection Questions:

1. How good are you at keeping your word? How can you be better?

___

___

___

___

2. Reflect on a time you didn't keep your word to someone. Did it affect your relationship? How did it make that person feel?

___

___

___

___

3. Reflect on a time someone didn't keep their word to you. Did it affect your relationship with them? How did it make you feel?

4. Have you ever talked a big game and not backed it up? How did it make you feel?

5. Do you view vows and promises differently? Explain what that difference is to you.

6. How important do you believe it is to keep your word to others?

NOTES

CHAPTER 30

IT'S OKAY NOT TO BE OKAY

Matthew 26:36–44

Overview:

Jesus prays and asks God if there is any way for Him to avoid His crucifixion.

Analysis:

If you needed any more proof that Jesus was human, look no further than this story. This was the final time Jesus prayed before He was betrayed. The text says He was "sorrowful and deeply distressed" (Matt. 26:37). My guy was hurting big time, and it shows that living a life pleasing to God is hard. Doing the things God needs you to do is hard, and it's okay to be affected by it. It's okay not to be okay.

I feel like a lot of Christians believe they need to suffer with a smile on their face. Regardless of what stresses and pains life throws your way, you think you have to put on a brave face. No, you don't. You can whine. You can complain. You can question. God didn't create us to be robots who blindly follow His orders. He gave us emotions. Don't feel like you are a bad Christian because you've had a bad day. Jesus was clearly having a bad day and needed to pray for the strength to continue on His path.

Jesus not only shows us it's okay to be emotional, but He also sets the example to be emotional in private. When John the Baptist was killed, He went to a deserted place (Matt. 14:1–12). When He was about to be betrayed, He went to the Garden in Gethsemane by Himself.

Separate yourself from others in times of emotional distress. Be alone. Take time for yourself to get your mind right before continuing the fight. Commune with God, and pray for His guidance and strength to endure your trials.

I believe the reason Jesus sets this example is because when we get emotional, we say and do things we don't mean. We take our pain out on others. Even in this story, Jesus snaps at His disciples for falling asleep while they were on watch (Matt. 26:40). Yes, you can say He did that because they didn't follow His orders and put their lives at risk, but I also believe His reaction was driven by His emotional state. He was still in the process of getting His mind right and was triggered when He found them asleep on the job.

My justification for this interpretation comes from the fact that His reaction to finding them asleep the second and third times was much tamer than the first. The second time, He didn't say anything to them. The third time, His energy was more like "Y'all still sleeping? I been praying for over an hour, and y'all still tired? Come on. We gotta go" (Matt. 26:43–44). It wasn't really an admonishment of their action like it was the first time around.

Now that I'm thinking about it, maybe He used them sleeping to gauge when He was mentally ready to go. I can imagine Him being livid the first time He saw them, taking a deep sigh, and saying, "I need to go pray some more." Then He went back to the garden. The second time feels like when you walk in on someone doing something you know makes you angry, but instead of saying something, you just walk away before doing something you regret. I picture Jesus taking a few steps out of the garden, hearing Peter snoring, and then saying, "Yep. Still mad" before heading back to the garden for His third and final time. The moral of the story is that it takes time to get your head on straight. Don't rush the process.

Conclusion:

The lesson we should take from this is the importance of mental health. When we aren't right in our mind, we aren't right in our actions. When we aren't right in our actions, innocent people get the brunt of our wrath.

There is nothing wrong with walking away from situations that trigger us when we are emotional. It's better to do that than act outside yourself. Your mind controls your temple—your body—so if you don't have control of your mind, you can't control your body. Your body will be controlled by your emotions. The only way to protect your temple is to protect and renew your mind.

Reflection Questions:

1. Have you ever suffered for the Lord? Did you feel the urge to put on a brave face even though you were hurting? How did it affect your spirit and the way you interacted with people?

___

___

___

___

___

2. Reflect on a time you popped off on someone when you were emotional. What were the results? How could you have handled the situation better?

___

___

___

___

___

3. List things you do to get your mind right. What are some things you would like to try?

___

___

___

___

___

NOTES

CHAPTER 31

BE BLAMELESS

Matthew 26:57–68

Overview:

Jesus has been captured. The religious leaders search for someone to provide a testimony that will justify sentencing Jesus to death. They find no one and wind up booking Him on a bogus blasphemy charge for not denying He was the Christ.

Analysis:

In the world of the Internet, it is almost impossible to avoid having skeletons in your closet. A post from five to 10 years ago can be viewed as problematic by today's standards and get you cancelled. Regardless, it's important to try to live life as blameless as possible. If you give your enemies an inch, they will take a mile. They will find a way to get you in trouble by any means necessary. Don't make their job easier by giving them ammunition.

Jesus lived His life blameless. The religious leaders could not find one person out of the multitudes He preached to who could give them just cause to crucify Him. Think about how crazy that is. Jesus preached to *thousands*, and not one person could say anything about Him that was worthy of a conviction. That is how we want to be. No matter how hard the enemy digs, they should continue to hit rocks instead of soil. Make 'em earn it.

Conclusion:

The second lesson in this story is that even if you manage to be blameless, sometimes you will still get got.

The enemy plays dirty. They don't have honor or integrity. As soon as the religious leaders created a reason to kill Jesus, they literally spat in His face and beat Him (Matt. 26:65–67). In that moment, their hatred and motives became clear as day.

They were looking for an excuse, not a reason, and unfortunately, that's the only thing people in a position of power need.

Jesus recognized this and handled Himself with dignity in the face of humiliation. He didn't stoop to their level, cause a scene, or beg for His life. That's what the enemy wants you to do. The enemy wants you to bow to their authority and grovel at their feet. They want you to feel like you're nothing. Don't give them the satisfaction. Keep your head up high, and trust that everything you are enduring is part of God's greater plan. He will give you the strength to withstand the adversity. There's always a light at the end of the tunnel.

Reflection Questions:

1. What are things you can do to start living a blameless life?

____

____

____

____

____

____

2. Have you ever been the subject of a witch hunt? What happened? Why do you think God allowed you to go through it?

____

____

____

____

____

____

NOTES

CHAPTER 32

TAKE IT ON THE CHEST

Matthew 27:11–14

Overview:

Jesus is brought in front of the governor, Pontius Pilate, for sentencing. The religious leaders present their accusations against Him, and Jesus's composure in the face of adversity impresses Pilate. He marveled at Jesus's ability to remain *silent* while being accused.

Analysis:

As stated in the previous chapter, there are people in the world who will find any excuse to take you down. The religious leaders had already decided they were going to find a way to get Jesus sentenced to death. His fate was sealed well before stepping in front of Pilate. There was no point in arguing with them. All fighting would have done was risk the religious leaders twisting His words to make Him look even more guilty.

If you are in the right, don't make yourself wrong by flapping your gums. You have to discern if a battle is worth fighting. If you feel like you've done all you can, accept your fate, and take it on the chest. Don't risk putting your foot in your mouth and making the situation worse. Again, the enemy is *looking* for reasons to justify their feelings about you, so all talking does is give them more opportunity to find fault with you.

It doesn't take much. You can say, "That's not true!" and they can respond, "Did you hear that hostile tone of voice? He's clearly guilty!" That type of ridiculous behavior will make you even more upset and fuel the urge you have to defend yourself, making the chances of saying something "incriminating" more likely. It's a vicious cycle. Control your tongue. Don't let it control you. Nine times out of 10, all fighting back will do is make the enemy look right about you.

Conclusion:

The above analysis is specifically referring to lose-lose situations. Someone has already decided you're guilty, and there is nothing you can do to change it. Save your breath. You will show more innocence by handling the situation with class instead of getting into a back and forth.

That is why I believe Pilate marveled at Jesus's silence. He was so used to seeing people beg for their lives and plead their cases that seeing Jesus take the accusations on the chest surprised him. It's what made him realize that Jesus was innocent and the victim of an envy-driven coup headed by the religious leaders (Matt. 27:18).

People are more perceptive than we often give them credit for. I can imagine the religious leaders getting visibly irritated at Jesus's lack of reaction as they accused Him. It's no fun to torment someone when the tormented doesn't squirm. When people are trying to hurt you, they want you to react.

When you don't react, it makes *them* angry, and that anger makes it clear there's a personal vendetta at play. That would explain how Pilate was able to perceive the religious leaders' jealousy.

People will show their tails if you give them the microphone and let them rift. What's done in the dark always comes to light. The easiest way to bring an adversary's true intentions to light is by allowing them to talk themselves into a corner.

Reflection Questions:

1. How difficult is it for you to bite your tongue? What do you think is the value of knowing when to keep your tongue in check?

____

____

____

____

2. Have you ever been in a lose-lose situation? How did you handle it?

____

____

____

____

3. Are you a person who fights to the bitter end? Why do you believe it's important to go out swinging? Discuss.

____

____

____

____

NOTES

CHAPTER 33

BEWARE THE HERD

Matthew 27:15–26

Overview:

Pilate is given the opportunity to release one of the prisoners. He wants to release Jesus because He knows He is innocent, but the religious leaders persuade the multitudes to ask for Barabbas (another prisoner) to be released. Pilate respects their request and sentences Jesus to be crucified.

Analysis:

The herd mentality is real. Jesus spent His entire adult life healing and teaching the multitudes, and how did they repay Him? They repaid Him by calling for His head because someone told them to. The text doesn't divulge what the religious leaders said, but I can almost guarantee it was a lot of "fake news."

We live in a time when you don't have to be right; you just have to be the first to post an opinion, and people will take it and run with it. A friend of mine posted about the death of a well-known celebrity, and I believed him. Without fact-checking, I told everyone in my office the news, and we all believed it until someone googled what the cause of death was, and no news outlet had reported it. It turned out to be a fake story.

In less than two minutes, one fake post had an office of 10 people believing a lie was the truth. Situations like this happen every day. It doesn't take much time or effort. The media has the power to create and push out narratives that will have you believing anything that generates the most buzz.

Nine times out of 10, negativity and controversy generates the biggest reaction. And if the controversy can be perceived as *offensive*, the social media mob will come after you. Take NBA Superstar Kyrie Irving, for example.

***Warning:* The following situation is a controversial topic. I'm using it as an example to illustrate the power of persuasion and nothing more.**

In 2022, Kyrie Irving posted a link to a documentary that contained anti-Semitic tropes. He didn't say anything about the documentary; he just posted the link to the film. The world went crazy like that Spongebob meme when his brain was on fire. Kyrie was suspended from playing basketball and could not return to work until he:

1. Apologized and condemned the documentary
2. Donated $500,000 to anti-hate causes
3. Received sensitivity *and* anti-Semitic training
4. Met with Jewish leaders and team management to demonstrate that he understood why what he did was wrong

On top of that, Kyrie lost several multi-million-dollar brand endorsements.

Again, all this man did was post a link. He didn't say anything about the film. In fact, when the reporter initially questioned Kyrie about it, he explicitly stated that he respects all cultures and religions, and just because he posted the link to the film doesn't mean he agrees with everything that was discussed in the film. The media wasn't satisfied with his answer and continued to ask him questions until he eventually got angry and popped off at a reporter who claimed he was promoting the film by posting it.

Guess which clip circulated on the Internet? It was the one where he popped off and was belligerent. In response to the video, countless social media warriors and TV personalities admonished him on their platforms, which is what led to his eventual punishment.

Whether or not you have a problem with what Kyrie did is inconsequential to the fact that the punishment did not fit the crime. For context, there have been several NBA players with assault charges and sexual misconduct accusations who didn't receive any form of punishment, so Kyrie having to go through a four-step recovery program for a tweet that had no legal implications is beyond excessive.

At worst, he should have been disciplined *in-house* and asked to make a public apology to the people he unintentionally offended. There was no reason for it to be such a public controversy when he stated that he didn't post it with malicious intent.

All the hoops he had to jump through and the finances he lost were unnecessary casualties, so how did it get that bad? The answer is "the herd." Once the herd sank their teeth into the story and voiced their disapproval, the NBA had no choice but to make an *example* out of Kyrie.

The crazy part is that a good number of the people who condemned him didn't watch his whole interview or the documentary itself to see if it was truly as bad as people were portraying it to be. They just ran with the narrative the media spun about the situation and based their opinions on that. That's the power of persuasion. A person can be force-fed an opinion and run with it without any understanding of what they are truly supporting.

That results in herd mentality and can lead to unfair decisions being made that negatively impact the alleged perpetrator.

Leaders don't want to be caught in the cross-hairs of controversy. It is much easier to fire an employee than it is to reason with an angry mob. It is much easier to throw the book at someone than it is to spend the time and effort required to give them a fair trial. After all, it doesn't affect them. It only affects the accused.

People are drawn toward taking the path of least resistance. That is why you need to be wary of the herd. If enough people ban together against you, they might take you down solely because it is easier to side with 10 people than it is to fight for one.

That's why Pilate released Barabbas instead of Jesus, and it's why Kyrie's punishment was so harsh. The herd is real, and it can swallow you up if you aren't careful.

Conclusion:

I'm not trying to be political. I'm just trying to open your eyes to the reality we live in. Another hard truth is that there is always someone profiting from the pain of others. For Jesus, it was the religious leaders. They gathered a herd to eliminate a man who had been a thorn in their side from the moment He hit the scene. His absence allowed them to be top dogs again. In the Kyrie situation, the media received significant revenue from the millions of views the story generated, and the film itself became a best seller on Amazon Prime Video and is still available for purchase to this very day. Neither parties truly cared about the harmfulness of the film; they only cared about the potential the story had to line their pockets.

The lesson here is that people with influence will do whatever they can to sway the opinion of the masses to suit their agenda. There is always an ulterior motive for gathering a herd. Remember this, and do whatever you can to take away their power. Both Pilate and Kyrie had opportunities to take power away from the herd, but they came up short due to the following reasons.

Pilate didn't "say it with his chest" (Chapter 7). He knew that killing Jesus was wrong, but he didn't stand on his principles. He bowed to the pressures of the crowd. If he followed what he knew was right, he would have told the crowd, "Unless you can provide me a compelling reason to crucify Jesus, we are going to release Him and crucify the known criminal Barabbas."

Kyrie didn't "take it on the chest" (Chapter 32). The reporters were clearly fishing for him to say something controversial, but instead of ending the conversation when he said, "I respect all religions," he kept responding to their questions and eventually gave them all the ammunition they needed to twist the situation into a news story that broke the Internet.

Finally, I want to briefly discuss a concept I call "herd faith." That is when people believe in an ideology because someone spoon-fed it to them. They didn't develop it on their own. As a Christian, don't allow your faith to follow a herd. Be a leader. Be a student of the faith. Have the curiosity to do the work, and study the Bible for yourself. If you don't, you are susceptible to joining a herd.

Look at your faith right now. How many of us have actually read the entire Bible—the basis of our faith and the thing we tell people we believe in wholeheartedly? I've read the book, and let me tell you there are some wild things in it, some things people might find problematic by today's standards. How can you adequately defend and share your beliefs if you don't truly know what you believe in? Don't have force-fed faith. Be a shepherd, not a sheep.

Reflection Questions:

1. Have you ever been attacked by a herd? Why? How did it end?

2. Have you ever been part of a herd? Why did you follow the crowd? Do you feel like you were right in doing so? Discuss.

3. List things you can do to prevent yourself from joining a herd.

4. Do you think you have "herd faith"? Why or why not? How can you be better at becoming a student of your faith?

NOTES

CHAPTER 34

YOU ARE NOT ALONE

Matthew 27:45

Overview:
Jesus's final words before His death on the cross.

Analysis:
For this final chapter, we are going to dive into Jesus's final words. Before Jesus died on the cross, He cried to the heavens, "My God, My God, why have you forsaken me?" (Matthew 27:46). In the literal sense, the word *forsaken* means abandoned or deserted.

In church, we are taught that God had to turn His back on Jesus and allow the crucifixion to take place so the prophecy could be fulfilled, but I find it interesting that Jesus specifically asked why God *abandoned* Him. He didn't ask, "Why am I the one who has to suffer?" or "Was this the only way?" He spoke from an *emotional* place. In that moment, He felt abandoned. He felt God had deserted Him. He felt alone on that cross.

The final lesson Jesus teaches us is that when we suffer for the Lord, it can feel lonely. It can feel like we are on an island by ourselves with no life boat. This feeling can lead to losing your faith, abusing drugs or alcohol, suicidal ideations, depression—the list goes on and on.

I'm here to tell you that you are *never* alone. I'm here to tell you that the Lord will *never* put more on you than you can bear (1 Cor. 10:13). Persevere, because what was once a trial can be transformed into a testimony—a story of triumph that can pull someone else out of the same situation. You may not see it in the present, but your current struggle might serve a greater purpose in the future.

"All things work together for good to those who love God, to those who are called according to His purpose" (Rom. 8:28).

So don't fear. Don't succumb to the darkness. Pray for a brighter day, and believe it will come. Cling to the ones you love. Be stronger than your situation, and hold on to your purpose.

We got this, baby. Peace and love.

Conclusion:

If you or someone you know is in need of emotional support, encourage them to reach out to a local pastor or call the suicide hotline—988. Contrary to its name, you don't have to have suicidal ideations to call them. They are there to talk and provide emotional support to anyone in need, so don't be afraid to make the call.

It takes a village, and if you are looking to find a tribe, use the QR code below or the link attached to your online purchase to join *The Village* Facebook group. Be blessed.

SUMMARY

Well, you did it! You made it all the way to the end. I hope the journey was enlightening, and I pray that you find value in the lessons presented in this book.

Keeping in line with the rest of the chapters, I will keep this summary short. You might have noticed a lot of recurring themes throughout the book. That is because all the lessons that Jesus's life taught us are connected. They aren't mutually exclusive. They rely and build on each other. Below are the hottest topics we discussed. They are in no particular order.

1. Maintaining humility
2. Doing things with the right intentions
3. Building, relying on, and supporting your village
4. Treating others the way you want to be treated
5. Utilizing discernment with the people you encounter on a day-to-day basis
6. Relying on God's strength instead of your own
7. Loving your fellow man
8. Haters gonna hate
9. Discerning God's calling for you
10. Becoming a mentor
11. It's okay to get emotional when you're hurting or struggling

12. Your enemies will prey on your downfall
13. Give your problems to God, and go to Him first
14. Be kind and compassionate
15. Be bold, be strong, and stand on your faith

This list is not all-encompassing, but you can use it as a basic summary of the key attributes for living a life like Christ.

That's all for now. Dream big, pray without ceasing, and elevate your faith. Take care.

NOTES

www.ingramcontent.com/pod-product-compliance
Lightning Source LLC
LaVergne TN
LVHW010613100826
845148LV00014B/2951